PRIVATE SECTOR OPERATIONS IN 2019

REPORT ON DEVELOPMENT EFFECTIVENESS

JULY 2020

ADB

ASIAN DEVELOPMENT BANK

Note:
In this publication, "$" refers to United States dollars.

Cover design and infographics by Jasper Lauzon.

Private sector operations in 2019. Cover photos represent some sectors that ADB committed financing to in 2019, such as agriculture, agribusiness, transport, energy (renewable energy including wind and solar), microfinance, equity funds, telecommunications, health, and education (photos from ADB; and Lu Guang, Eric Sales, JSC Evex Hospitals, Kacific Broadband Satellites Group [Kacific], BTS, AC Energy for ADB).

CONTENTS

TABLES, FIGURES, AND BOXES

FOREWORD

The Asia and Pacific region has made great strides toward meeting its development objectives in the past decades. The Asian Development Bank (ADB) has been a key partner in the significant transformation of the region and is committed to continue serving the region in the next phase of its development. Old challenges such as income inequality and social disparity continue to be the cause of many development problems even in the highly developed economies in the region. However, new challenges are also throwing the development trajectory off course. Chief among these is the ongoing coronavirus disease or COVID-19 pandemic, which has exposed low-income families in the region to their most vulnerable situation.

To craft the new way forward, we need to focus on areas that are proving to be vital in the present. For example, inclusive finance is an area through which women and marginalized sectors have been empowered and given a stronger voice. Similarly, support for microenterprises has helped lift people out of poverty. Addressing climate change has also been identified as key to delivering sustainable solutions. These are some of the areas that ADB, through its private sector operations, committed financing to in 2019.

In 2019, ADB also prepared its Operational Plan for Private Sector Operations, 2019–2024. This was endorsed by the Board in January 2020. The plan focuses on scaling up ADB's private sector operations in health, agribusiness, and education. It envisages that ADB will continue supporting core infrastructure and finance sector investments while also venturing into areas of infrastructure beyond energy, such as environmental infrastructure, transport, and information and communication technology. ADB will also be expanding into new and frontier markets.

As the pandemic hobbles and continues to negatively impact the private sector in the region, ADB is working with governments and private sector clients to ensure that the countries and businesses rebound from external shocks. Already, ADB is responding to the pandemic by supporting its developing member countries through finance, knowledge, and partnerships. It has approved a series of measures to streamline its operations for quicker and more flexible delivery of assistance. Some $2 billion from ADB's $20 billion COVID-19 response package is focused on the private sector to help clients in developing member countries counter the severe macroeconomic impacts from the pandemic. The package will provide loans and guarantees for financial institutions to rejuvenate trade and supply chains. Enhanced microfinance loan and guarantee support and a facility to provide liquidity to small and medium-sized enterprises, including those run by female entrepreneurs, will also be implemented alongside direct financing of companies responding to, or impacted by, COVID-19.

ADB will continue to devise innovative approaches and apply critical thinking to maximize the potential of private enterprise to address the challenges facing the region. It is set to expand private sector operations to reach one-third of its total operations in terms of number of projects by 2024. Solid progress has been made in 2019 toward this target, when ADB committed a record-high number of private sector investments for 38 projects, covering 16 different developing member countries and including 7 regional projects.

Projects committed in 2019 totaled over $3 billion, and ADB mobilized $6.98 billion in private sector cofinancing, almost half of which was long-term cofinancing. In the coming years, ADB will be enhancing its local currency offerings and further developing its equity investments platform. Guided by the new 5-year operational plan for its private sector operations, ADB will mobilize more financial resources through credit enhancement, syndications, and asset management activities.

These are some of the key building blocks needed to achieve the overall development agenda for ADB, its stakeholders, and its partners in the months and years ahead. In all of this, the private sector must assume a stronger role—to help ADB expand its vision of achieving *a prosperous, inclusive, resilient, and sustainable Asia and the Pacific*, while sustaining its efforts to eradicate extreme poverty.

I invite everyone to examine this *Private Sector Operations in 2019—Report on Development Effectiveness*, as now, more than ever, we need to inform stakeholders and partners, share best practices, and learn from each other's development experiences. We welcome your feedback and continued participation as we engage more of the private sector in development and economic recovery.

DIWAKAR GUPTA
Vice-President, Private Sector Operations and Public–Private Partnerships
Asian Development Bank

PREFACE

In January 2020, the Board of Directors of the Asian Development Bank (ADB) endorsed the Operational Plan for Private Sector Operations, 2019–2024. ADB will further sharpen the focus of its private sector operations with an increasing share of complex, highly innovative, smaller, and riskier projects in challenging markets and sectors; and will enhance its already considerable efforts to address climate change and support women under an operational plan that will guide ADB's nonsovereign assistance over the next 5 years.

The plan lays out a comprehensive outline of critical planned initiatives to achieve the objectives of Strategy 2030, including the growth of private sector operations overall and a major increase in the commercial financing that we mobilize. Through its private sector operations, ADB will be leading by example, investing in developmentally impactful projects with a focus on more challenging sectors such as agribusiness, education, health, and areas of infrastructure beyond energy; including geographies such as fragile and conflict-affected situations, small island developing states, and less developed member countries. The plan envisions more tailored debt and guarantee products, broader local currency offerings and reinforced equity operations, and an integrated One ADB approach to effectively and efficiently support the private sector, with the Private Sector Operations Department (PSOD) working jointly with other ADB departments.

With a new operational plan and focus, beginning with this edition, this series of annual reports is being retitled *Private Sector Operations—Report on Development Effectiveness*, and will review and highlight the development effectiveness of ADB's private sector operations. The series reports on active PSOD projects and their performance in achieving agreed targets and expected results. This year's report is the 10th edition and features ADB's private sector operations' development results in 2019, major contributions to ADB's new corporate results framework and Strategy 2030, contributions to realizing the Sustainable Development Goals (SDGs), and to the new operational plan.

The report was prepared by a core PSOD team led by Gloria Paniagua, Senior Results Management Specialist, Development Effectiveness Team, Private Sector Transaction Support Division. The report benefited from the guidance of Christopher Thieme, Deputy Director General. Team members included Ulritz Uzein Corcuera, Associate Economics Officer, for technical and research support; Ma. Cherriemae Belo Bejo, Development Effectiveness Consultant, for results data aggregation; Christian Lapie Abeleda, Associate Project Analyst, for project contribution to Strategy 2030 operational priorities; Jamie Kho, Senior Investment Officer for verification of operational results; Abraham B. Villanueva, ADB Cartographer, for design of the PSOD commitment map; and Christhel Anne Agulay Villaruel, Operations Assistant, for administrative assistance. Consultants Cherry Lynn Zafaralla edited the report, Alvin Tubio performed typesetting, and Jasper Lauzon designed the cover and infographics. The Department of Communications planned and coordinated the dissemination of the report, while the Office of Administrative Services printed the report.

PSOD also acknowledges the review comments and inputs from Mark Kunzer, Director, Private Sector Transaction Support Division; Shantanu Chakraborty, Director, Infrastructure Finance Division 1 (Central and West Asia, South Asia); Jackie Surtani, Director, Infrastructure Finance Division 2 (East Asia, Southeast Asia, The Pacific); Christine Engstrom, Director, Financial Institution Division; Janette Hall, Director, Investment Funds and Special Initiatives Division; Steven Beck, Advisor and Head of Trade and Supply Chain Finance; Martin Lemoine, Unit Head, Food and Agribusiness Investment Team; Aniruddha Patil, Unit Head, Health and Education Investments; and Bart Raemaekers, Advisor and Head, Guarantees and Syndications Unit.

MICHAEL BARROW
Director General, Private Sector Operations Department

ABBREVIATIONS

ADB	Asian Development Bank
ASEAN	Association of Southeast Asian Nations
DMC	developing member country
FCAS	fragile and conflict-affected situations
ICT	information and communication technology
LEAP	Leading Asia's Private Sector Infrastructure Fund
MSMEs	micro, small, and medium-sized enterprises
PRC	People's Republic of China
PREP	Pacific Renewable Energy Program
PSOD	Private Sector Operations Department
SDGs	Sustainable Development Goals
SMEs	small and medium-sized enterprises
TFP	Trade Finance Program
WTE	waste-to-energy
XARR	extended annual review report

WEIGHTS AND MEASURES

tCO_2e	tons of carbon dioxide equivalent
GWh	gigawatt-hour
m^3	cubic meter
MW	megawatt
t	ton

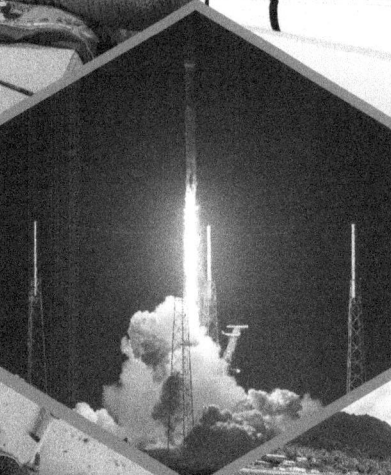

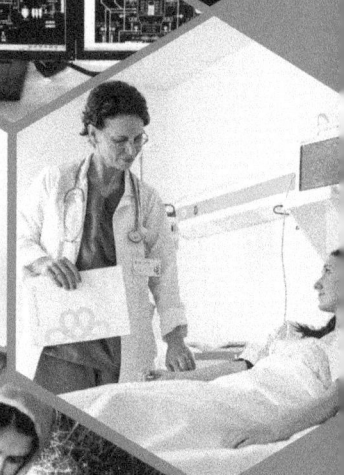

EXECUTIVE SUMMARY

Achieving the Asian Development Bank's (ADB) Strategy 2030 will require significant contributions by the private sector. The public sector currently provides over 90% of the region's infrastructure investment, but the private sector has a key role in filling the region's investment needs, estimated at around $460 billion annually from 2016 until 2020. Private sector investments are particularly important in the power generation and telecommunications sectors. Access to finance in the region remains constrained due to underdeveloped markets. An ADB policy brief from its 2019 Trade Finance Gaps, Growth, and Jobs Survey reported that the global trade finance gap remains at $1.5 trillion, with access to trade finance disproportionately skewed in favor of large firms despite the high demand from small and medium-sized enterprises (SMEs), especially in Asia and the Pacific.

ADB has set a target to expand private sector operations to reach one-third of total operations in number by 2024. Solid progress was made on this undertaking in 2019, when ADB committed private sector investments for 38 projects (this is a 19% increase compared to the 32 projects committed in 2018)—the highest number of projects committed since ADB's first private sector financing undertaking in 1983. ADB's private sector portfolio grew by 11% from 2018 to $13.6 billion in 2019. The 2019 new commitments across 16 developing member countries (DMCs) plus 7 regional projects totaled $3.0 billion. In 2019, ADB generated a record $6.98 billion in commercial cofinancing, almost half of which was long-term cofinancing; and mobilized $125 million from transaction advisory services.

Programs managed by the ADB Private Sector Operations Department (PSOD) achieved record volumes in 2019. Women, in particular, benefited significantly from the Microfinance Risk Participation and Guarantee Program, which facilitated $274.3 million in local currency loans to microfinance institutions throughout the region for on-lending to low-income borrowers. Small and medium-sized enterprises also benefited through the Trade Finance Program (TFP), which supported 4,069 SME transactions. Meanwhile, banks were able to play a part in helping close market gaps for trade finance—estimated in 2019 to be $1.5 trillion globally—through the TFP's guarantees and loans. The TFP facilitated a total of 4,832 transactions supporting cross-border trade finance, of which 3,731 were intraregional transactions, and 1,361 involved trade between DMCs. The TFP's total 2019 transactions were valued at $5.4 billion, of which $3.5 billion was cofinanced by banks, private insurers, and official agencies. Among the 21 countries covered by the TFP, the most active in 2019 were Armenia, Bangladesh, Pakistan, Sri Lanka, and Viet Nam.

Meanwhile, ADB's Supply Chain Finance Program also supported SMEs, by facilitating 448 SME transactions, or 78% of 577 total transactions (all intraregional) in 2019. The 577 total transactions were valued at $118.7 million, with $59.3 million cofinanced by partner financial institutions. This program complements the TFP by assuming corporate risk and developing both domestic and cross-border trade.

In pursuit of Strategy 2030 key strategic priorities, the ADB PSOD activities in 2019 had the following features:

- 82% of commitments contained specific gender elements;
- 42% of the committed projects were in frontier economies;
- $722 million was committed for climate-related activities, expected to avoid 7.6 million tons of carbon dioxide equivalent emissions;
- 26% of the committed transactions amounting to $345.7 million aimed to provide sustainable and affordable clean energy; and
- 36% of the total commitment amount in 2019 was dedicated to the transport sector for 108 million passengers (yearly) to have convenient and efficient transportation.

Expected Results of Projects Committed in 2019

Transactions committed in 2019 will make significant contributions to the economies of ADB's DMCs. They are expected to generate more than $532 million in government revenues and enable procurement of $2.1 billion worth of goods and services from local firms. The commitments in 2019 are expected to generate 24,273 new jobs.

These transactions will provide access to financial services to almost 2.7 million individuals as well as micro, small, and medium-sized enterprises (MSMEs). Over 96% of these MSMEs are expected to be women or enterprises owned by women. Agribusiness projects committed in 2019 are designed to help improve the livelihood of approximately 12,400 farmers. In addition to improving rural livelihoods, these transactions will also contribute to improved food security.

Transactions committed in 2019 will improve access to infrastructure services in DMCs. They will generate some 27,616 gigawatt-hours of energy annually, enough to serve 2.1 million average households in Asia. Private sector operations committed in 2019 will also help provide an efficient and reliable mass transportation to 108 million passengers once fully operational.

Results Delivered

Active private sector operations in 2019 have contributed to national economies by purchasing local goods and services worth around $13.8 billion and contributing $9.5 billion in government revenues. Projects have provided employment for an additional 319,743 people, and trained 422,830 beneficiaries, mostly on responsible finance. ADB's private sector clients have achieved emissions reductions of 30.7 million tons of carbon dioxide equivalent annually.

Active projects report having installed 19,518 megawatts in electrical generation capacity, with total power generated of 36,358 gigawatt-hours, enough to power 2.7 million typical homes in Asia. ADB's private sector clients have treated 1.1 billion cubic meters of wastewater and produced 875 million cubic meters of drinking water.

Active projects are supporting access to finance for over 33.2 million individuals and MSMEs, of which 74% are women or enterprises owned by women. Projects contributed to improving the livelihood of 1.5 million farmers either through inclusion in agribusiness supply chains, or through financial inclusion of small-scale farmers and farming households. Other projects contributed to the education of 35,568 additional students.

Conclusion

ADB's private sector operations have grown significantly and are expected to grow even more in the coming years. PSOD will continue this trajectory by expanding its business both geographically and in sectors where it has been less active. Since PSOD began reporting development results in 2010, ongoing operations have achieved significant progress in terms of development impact. PSOD pledges to carry on this trend and to continue delivering impactful results in the Asia and Pacific region.

PRIVATE SECTOR OPERATIONS DEPARTMEN
COMMITMENTS, 2019

38 projects, $3.0 billic

Kazakhstan, $41 million
- Total Eren Access M-KAT Solar Power
- Baikonyr Solar Power

Armenia, $44 million
- Yerevan Gas-fired Combined-Cycle Power Plant

Georgia, $29 million
- Low-Income Housing Finance
- Hospital Bond Project

Afghanistan, $4 million
- Kandahar Solar Power

Pakistan, $15 million
- Expanding Access to Credit for Women

India, $965 million
- Avaada Solar Project
- Railways Track Electrification Project
- Highway Equipment Finance
- Expanding Micro, Small, Medium-Sized Enterprise Lending
- Tata Capital Growth II
- Supporting Access to Finance for Women in Rural Areas (2018)

Nepal, $30 million
- Upper Trishuli 1 Hydro Power

Bangladesh, $14 million
- Second PRAN Agribusiness

Thailand, $459 million
- Bangkok Mass Rapid Transit Project (Pink and Yellow Lines)
- Energy Absolute Green Bond for Wind Power Project
- Eastern Economic Corridor Independent Power Project

Regional,* $163 million
- Capital Contribution in Credit Guarantee and Investment Facility
- Everbridge Partners Fund I, L.P.
- Kaizen Private Equity II Pte. Ltd.
- Tertiary Education
- AC Energy Green Bond
- Inclusive Beverage Production and Distribution Pro
- Asia-Pacific Remote Broadband Internet Satellite

* The regional projects extend across the following countries: Bangladesh, Brunei Darussalam, Cambodia, the People's Republic of China, Fiji, India, Indonesia, Kazakhstan, Kiribati, the Kyrgyz Republic, the Lao People's Democratic Republic, Malaysia, Myanmar, Nepal, Niue, Papua New Guinea, the Philippines, Singapore, Solomon Islands, Sri Lanka, Thailand, Timor-Leste, Tonga, Tuvalu, Vanuatu, and Viet Nam.

People's Republic of China, $381 million
- Healthcare Leasing in Underdeveloped Regions
- Eco-Industrial Park Waste-to-Energy
- CDH VGC Fund II, L.P.
- Industrial and Municipal Wastewater Treatment
- Integrated and Sustainable Livestock Value Chain

Mongolia, $47 million
- Sermsang Khushig Kundi Solar
- MSME Financing
- Gender Inclusive Dairy Value Chain

Myanmar, $597 million
- Nationwide Data Connectivity
- Myingyan Natural Gas Power (2017)

Viet Nam, $18 million
- Floating Solar Energy Project

Philippines, $30 million
- Fostering Women's Empowerment Through Financial Inclusion in Conflict-Impacted and Lagging Provinces

Papua New Guinea, $10 million
- Supporting Inclusive Finance through the Development of Private Sector Banking

Indonesia, $153 million
- Riau Natural Gas Power
- High-Value Coconut Processing Project

- Agriculture
- Health
- Education
- Clean Energy
- Energy (Other)
- Information and Communication Technology
- Finance
- Transport
- Water and Other Urban Infrastructure Services

This map was produced by the cartography unit of the Asian Development Bank. The boundaries, colors, denominations, and any other information shown on this map do not imply, on the part of the Asian Development Bank, any judgment on the legal status of any territory, or any endorsement or acceptance of such boundaries, colors, denominations, or information.

Results Expected from Projects Committed in 2019

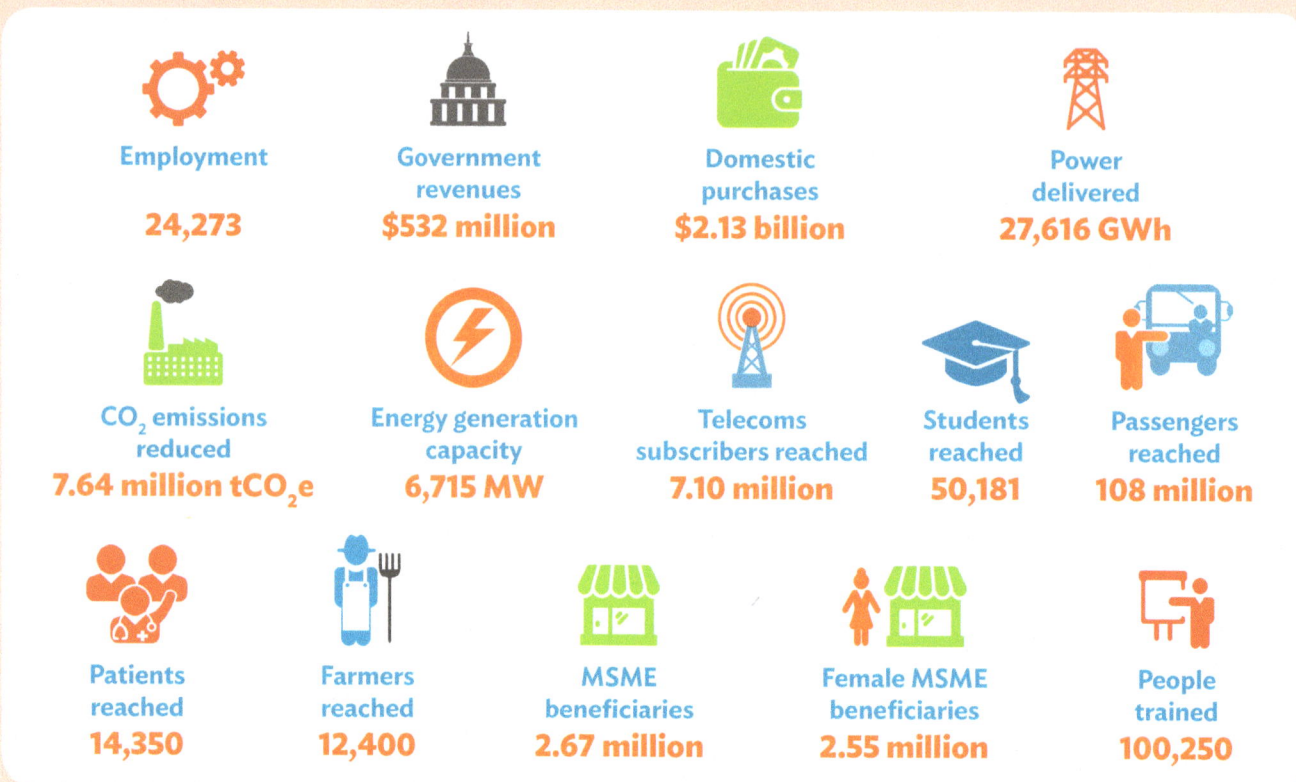

Employment
24,273

Government revenues
$532 million

Domestic purchases
$2.13 billion

Power delivered
27,616 GWh

CO_2 emissions reduced
7.64 million tCO_2e

Energy generation capacity
6,715 MW

Telecoms subscribers reached
7.10 million

Students reached
50,181

Passengers reached
108 million

Patients reached
14,350

Farmers reached
12,400

MSME beneficiaries
2.67 million

Female MSME beneficiaries
2.55 million

People trained
100,250

Results Achieved by PSOD's Active Portfolio

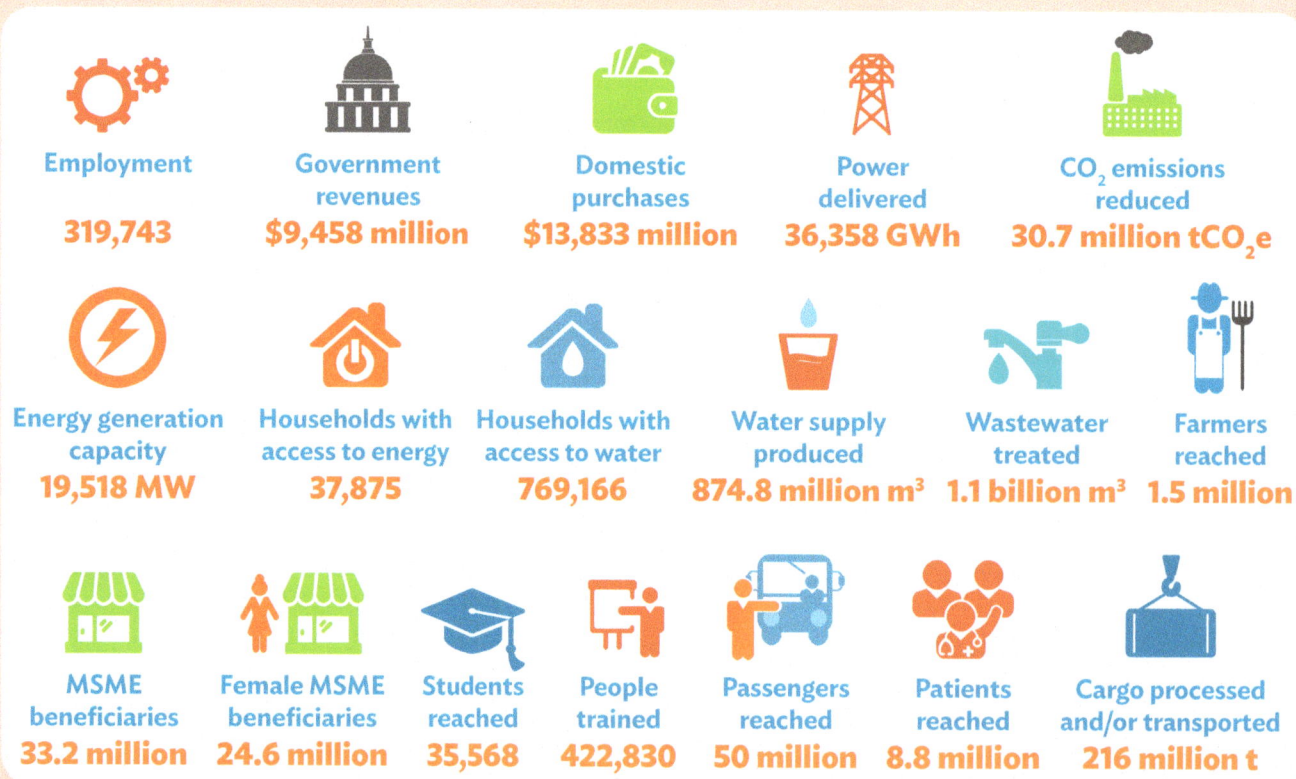

Employment
319,743

Government revenues
$9,458 million

Domestic purchases
$13,833 million

Power delivered
36,358 GWh

CO_2 emissions reduced
30.7 million tCO_2e

Energy generation capacity
19,518 MW

Households with access to energy
37,875

Households with access to water
769,166

Water supply produced
874.8 million m^3

Wastewater treated
1.1 billion m^3

Farmers reached
1.5 million

MSME beneficiaries
33.2 million

Female MSME beneficiaries
24.6 million

Students reached
35,568

People trained
422,830

Passengers reached
50 million

Patients reached
8.8 million

Cargo processed and/or transported
216 million t

CO_2 = carbon dioxide; tCO_2e = tons of carbon dioxide equivalent; GWh = gigawatt-hour; m^3 = cubic meter; MSME = micro, small, and medium-sized enterprise; MW = megawatt; PSOD = Private Sector Operations Department; t = ton.
Source: Asian Development Bank (Private Sector Operations Department).

▲ **A 135-megawatt solar power plant in Kazakhstan.** ADB will continue to focus on delivering green, sustainable, resilient, and inclusive energy infrastructure to sustainably meet the growing demand for energy in the region (photo by M-Kat Green LLP).

INTRODUCTION

The Asia and Pacific region continues to sustain moderate growth while keeping development inclusive for all. Weaker global growth in 2019 due to continuing global trade tensions and weakening domestic investments have tempered the region's economic growth prospects. The Asian Development Bank (ADB) reports that developing Asia's gross domestic product (GDP) growth decelerated to 5.2% in 2019 from a high of 5.9% in 2018.[1]

Despite the weaker growth, the region has made some progress. Over the past 2 decades, the region's share of global GDP at purchasing power parity has grown from 30.3% in 2000 to a robust 42.8% in 2018, a 0.2% rise from the previous year and equivalent to above one-third of global GDP.[2] Among the biggest economies in the region, Indonesia posted the third fastest GDP growth rate at 5.2%, next to the People's Republic of China (PRC) and India. Collectively, the trickle-down effect of economic growth in the region was evident as manifested in its declining poverty incidence.

According to the World Bank, the absolute number of people in the region living on extreme poverty or earning less than $1.90 a day at 2011 purchasing power parity has declined to 263 million from 1.1 billion people in 2002.[3]

[1] ADB. 2020. *Asian Development Outlook 2020.* Manila. https://www.adb.org/publications/asian-development-outlook-2020-innovation-asia.

[2] ADB. 2019. *Key Indicators for Asia and the Pacific 2019.* Manila. https://www.adb.org/publications/key-indicators-asia-and-pacific-2019.

[3] ADB estimates using data from the World Bank's PovcalNet Database. http://iresearch.worldbank.org/PovcalNet/home.aspx (accessed 27 March 2020).

In no small measure, part of this positive development has been a result of the efforts of the private sector—the engine that drives economic growth in most market-based economies. Thus, governments should continue to put in place an enabling policy environment that allows businesses to prosper and stimulate economic activity.

Many Asian economies face important medium-term challenges requiring structural reforms.[4] Governments understand the need for public policy that calls for dynamic solutions to address increasingly complex and emerging development challenges. With many of the economic and social solutions demanding fiscal resources beyond a nation's effective capacity, an optimal blend of public and private investments becomes essential. Leveraging private sector capital is seen as a critical ingredient in addressing many of the pressing challenges in the region.

In its long-term corporate Strategy 2030, ADB seeks to eradicate extreme poverty and achieve a prosperous, inclusive, resilient, and sustainable Asia and the Pacific.[5] The private sector is highlighted as critical to achieving its goals in the new strategy, and ADB is targeting to expand the number of private sector operations to reach one-third of its total operations by 2024. ADB also aims to attract $2.50 of long-term cofinancing for every $1.00 of its own financing for private sector operations by 2030.

In 2019, ADB prepared the Operational Plan for Private Sector Operations, 2019–2024, which was endorsed by the Board in January 2020.

Aligned with Strategy 2030, the plan outlines how ADB will continue to support core infrastructure and financial investments; and expand opportunities in agribusiness, education, health, as well as in infrastructure projects beyond the energy sector. Attention will continue to focus on fragile and conflict-affected situations (FCAS), small island developing states, and low-income developing member countries (DMCs). In middle-income and upper-middle income countries, ADB will take a targeted approach, focusing on underserved and disadvantaged areas.

The operational plan recognizes the need to further expand and diversify private sector operations. Thus, ADB has established operational targets based on number and quality of transactions, rather than conventional monetary value. Under the operational plan, the private sector will be tapped through ADB's various credit enhancement products, third-party funding platforms for co-investment, and public–private partnerships for private initiative to have stronger participation in financing development.

In 2020, the teams that guide ADB's private sector operations will continue to devise innovative approaches and apply critical thinking to maximize the potential of private enterprise to address key development challenges, in particular the global COVID-19 pandemic. ADB will remain steadfast in its commitment to pursue development impact as a key objective of its private sector operations, ensuring profitability and commercial sustainability, as commercial success is correlated with development outcomes.

---

[4] World Bank and International Monetary Fund. 2018. *Regional Economic Outlook: Asia Pacific.* https://www.imf.org/en/Publications/REO/APAC/Issues/2018/04/16/areo0509.

[5] ADB. 2018. *Asian Development Bank Strategy 2030: Achieving a Prosperous, Inclusive, Resilient, and Sustainable Asia and the Pacific.* Manila. https://www.adb.org/documents/strategy-2030-prosperous-inclusive-resilient-sustainable-asia-pacific.

▲ **ADB's first satellite financing.** The Asia-Pacific Remote Broadband Internet Satellite Project provides wide access to broadband internet connections to remote areas where internet coverage is limited (photos by Kacific).

OPERATIONAL RESULTS

The Private Sector Operations Department (PSOD) of ADB promotes strong partnerships with private enterprises and other financing institutions to develop robust and highly developmental transactions in the Asia and Pacific region. To attract and mobilize financing, PSOD leverages on its diversified financing modalities by scaling on its different lending instruments and blended financing structures, among many others. PSOD also provides support through equity investments and debt securities to selected high-growth platforms to fill in the financing needs of the market.

In recent years, the average time between approval and first signature of financing agreements has been 4 months. As a result, the cohort of projects approved and those committed (signed) in 2019 partially consist of different projects as a project may be approved in one year and signed in the next.[6]

New Projects Committed in 2019

ADB is moving toward a more focused private sector operations with emphasis on quality transactions with high development impact. In 2019, ADB's Board of Directors approved 35 nonsovereign projects for a total amount of $1.64 billion (Figure 1). PSOD committed 38 transactions for a total of $3.0 billion (Figure 2). While the overall approval amount decreased by 55%, the number of commitments increased by 19% compared to 2018. The number of projects committed in 2019 are the highest achieved by PSOD to date, exceeding the projection for the year. This signified a more diversified private sector portfolio while being able to expand ADB's support to private businesses in over 16 countries across the region. This expansion enables ADB to provide support in more challenging sectors and capture the underserved markets on a wider geographic spectrum.

---

[6] Committed project refers to a project for which a legal agreement has been signed. Committed amounts refer to the total amount for which legal agreements have been signed.

Figure 1: Private Sector Project Approvals, 2015–2019

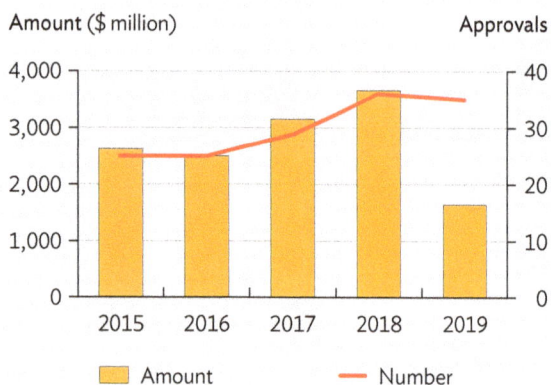

Source: Asian Development Bank (Private Sector Operations Department).

Figure 2: Private Sector Project Commitments, 2015–2019

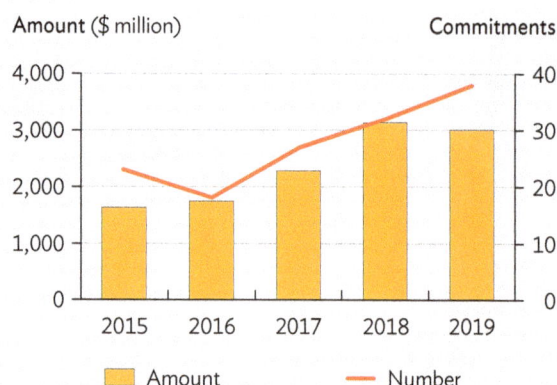

Source: Asian Development Bank (Private Sector Operations Department).

Private sector operations represent almost 60% of the total cofinancing mobilized by ADB. In 2019, direct value-added cofinancing decreased from $7.2 in 2018 to $7.0 billion, of which $187.4 million came from official cofinancing contributed by member governments and administered by ADB (Table 1). ADB's Trade and Supply Chain Financing Programs contributed $3.6 billion, with the remainder consisting of B loans, guarantees, parallel loans, and risk transfers.

For the past 5 years, South Asia has received the largest amount of financing committed, with majority of new investments concentrated in India through a mix of infrastructure, agriculture, financial, and equity fund projects. Most notable among the new committed projects in India are (i) the electrification of 3,378 kilometers (km) of railway track, which is expected to move millions of new passengers and increase the volume of cargo freight to be transported within the country; and (ii) a debt financing project to support the growth of micro, small, and medium-sized enterprises (MSMEs), by providing financial products and services to a portion of underserved segments consisting of around 1.6 million new MSME borrowers, 1.5 million of whom are women borrowers.

Table 1: Value-Added Cofinancing, 2019 ($ million)

	Amount
Official Cofinancing Generated by PSOD	187.35
Commercial Cofinancing	6,780.81
B Loans	181.50
Guarantee Cofinancing	138.12
Parallel Loans and/or Equity	2,256.33
Risk Transfer Arrangements	649.26
Trade Finance	3,496.27
Supply Chain Finance	59.33
Direct Value-Added Cofinancing	6,968.16

PSOD = Private Sector Operations Department.

Note: Amount excludes technical assistance cofinancing.

Source: Asian Development Bank (Private Sector Operations Department).

In Southeast Asia, ADB's new committed investments are largely dominated by infrastructure projects, particularly on transport, information and communication technology (ICT), and energy, owing to the region's huge infrastructure deficit. These new projects, spread across Indonesia, Myanmar, the Philippines, Thailand, and Viet Nam, will provide people with improved access to sustainable energy, reliable and efficient transportation, and stronger financial inclusion for women.

Also, PSOD is committed to provide innovative finance for private sector projects that spur regional cooperation to encourage enterprises to replicate successful business practices.

A total of $845 million has been committed by ADB to regional projects across the region, where one of the new projects aims to advance the development of the education sector through a Tertiary Education Project.[7] Pacific projects amounting to $12 million will reach out to beneficiaries across Papua New Guinea and Samoa (Figure 3).

In 2019, transport projects dominated the commitment portfolio of PSOD amounting to $1.1 billion, 98% of which will be invested in (i) a railway electrification project in India, which is expected to help increase the number of passengers and cargo to be transported annually; and (ii) a mass rapid transit project in Thailand, which will improve the lives of urban commuters while generating thousands of jobs. ADB also committed $685 million for new energy projects, one of which is to support the construction and operation of a portfolio of waste-to-energy (WTE) plants in the PRC using clean and state-of-the-art technology that can meet stringent environmental standards.

Commitments to direct financial institutions amounted to $581 million, representing 13 new transactions in over seven countries across the region. The investments will enable financial institutions to continue lending to certain high-development segments such as women borrowers and microenterprises. ADB has committed $525 million for projects in the ICT sector, while health and education accounted for $19 million of total commitments (Figure 4).

Figure 3: Commitments by Region, 2015–2019
($ billion)

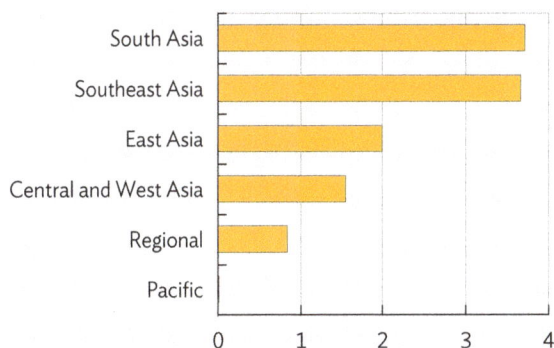

Source: Asian Development Bank (Private Sector Operations Department).

Figure 4: Commitments by Sector, 2015–2019
($ billion)

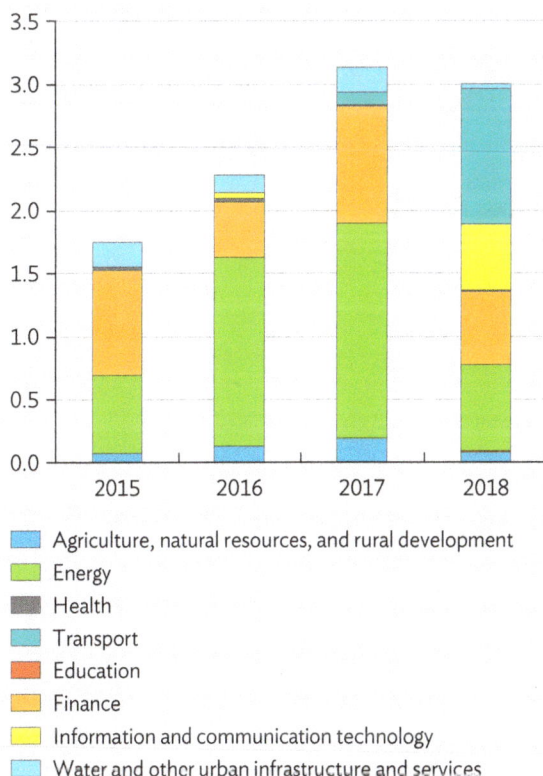

Agriculture, natural resources, and rural development
Energy
Health
Transport
Education
Finance
Information and communication technology
Water and other urban infrastructure and services

Source: Asian Development Bank (Private Sector Operations Department).

---

[7] The regional projects cover the following countries: Bangladesh, Brunei Darussalam, Cambodia, the People's Republic of China, Fiji, India, Indonesia, Kazakhstan, Kiribati, the Kyrgyz Republic, the Lao People's Democratic Republic, Malaysia, Myanmar, Nepal, Niue, Papua New Guinea, the Philippines, Singapore, Solomon Islands, Sri Lanka, Thailand, Timor-Leste, Tonga, Tuvalu, Vanuatu, and Viet Nam.

Box 1
Trade Finance Knowledge Products —How They Enhance Impact on Developing Asia

The Trade Finance Program (TFP) supported almost 5,000 transactions in 2019 valued at $5.4 billion, boosting growth and creating jobs in developing Asia. Apart from this monetary value, its knowledge work also promotes meaningful change.

Gender: TFP's award-winning Gender Initiative analyzed the human resource policies of 19 banks to identify enhancements that would attract, retain, and promote more women in banking. Twelve banks implemented 25 recommendations.

Digitization: In partnership with the Government of Singapore and the International Chamber of Commerce, TFP established the Digital Trade Standards Initiative to create the protocols and standards that will drive interoperability throughout the trade ecosystem. This will create efficiencies and productivity, and lower barriers to entry for small and medium-sized enterprises (SMEs).

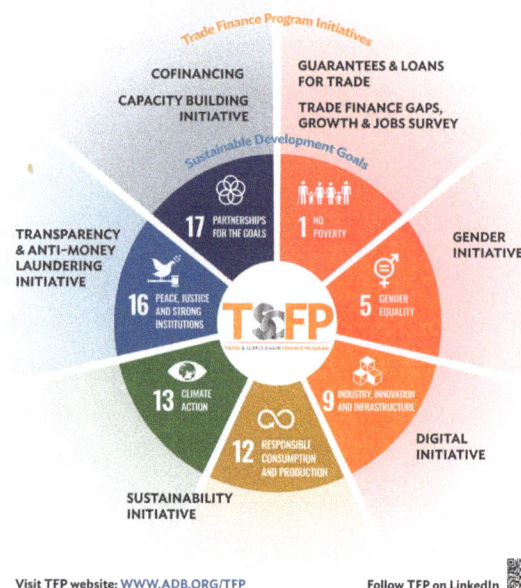

Trade & Supply Chain Finance Program
delivering SUSTAINABLE DEVELOPMENT GOALS

ADB's Trade Finance Program empowers countries to meet the Sustainable Development Goals by closing market gaps through guarantees, loans, and knowledge products.

Since 2009, the TFP has supported $41.7 billion in trade across 25,915 transactions (70% SME related).

Visit TFP website: WWW.ADB.ORG/TFP   Follow TFP on LinkedIn

Anti-money laundering: TFP's Transparency Initiative has two objectives: prevent criminal activity in the financial system; and reduce the unintended consequences of regulations that contribute to SME financing gaps. TFP brought public and private sectors together to develop proposals that will (i) streamline anti-money laundering processes to reduce unintended consequences from regulations, and (ii) help create more robust law enforcement. In addition, TFP provides partner banks with online training in anti-money laundering and counter terrorism financing.

Source: Asian Development Bank (Private Sector Operations Department).

PSOD's programs also achieved record volumes with the Microfinance Risk Participation and Guarantee Program in 2019, facilitating $274.3 million in local currency loans to microfinance institutions for low-income borrowers, primarily women, throughout the region. The average size of loan to micro borrowers is $250. The Trade Finance Program (TFP) financed $5.4 billion in transactions (Box 1), including $3.5 billion in cofinancing, while deals supported by the Supply Chain Finance Program amounted to $119 million for small and medium-sized enterprises (SMEs), half of it cofinanced.

PSOD continued to diversify its use of financial products in 2019 (Figure 5). Loan products still accounted for the bulk of the product mix in 2019, constituting 89% of total committed funding. ADB's equity products represented 5%, while guarantees investments grew to 6% compared to 2018. ADB's financing of a railways track electrification project in India and a telecommunications nationwide data connectivity lending project in Myanmar contributed significantly to the total loan commitments.

Figure 5: Commitments by Product, 2015–2019
($ billion)

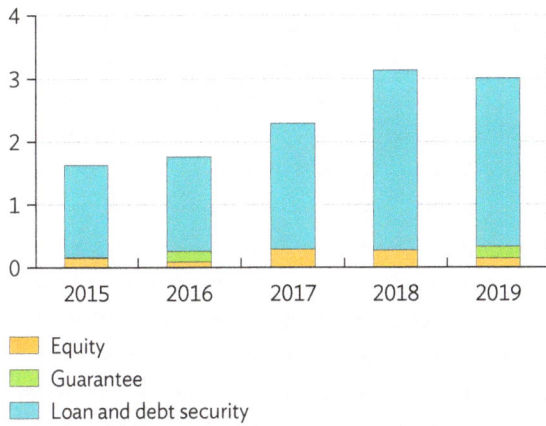

Equity
Guarantee
Loan and debt security

Source: Asian Development Bank (Private Sector Operations Department).

Portfolio of Projects under Implementation

The total committed portfolio of PSOD, consisting of outstanding amounts and funds committed but not yet disbursed, grew by 11% to $13.6 billion in 2019 (Figure 6).

Figure 7 shows the regions with the largest share in PSOD's portfolio, led by Southeast Asia (38%) and South Asia (28%). Some 25% of the portfolio were clients operating in frontier countries.[8]

In 2019, the disbursement ratio jumped to 39.3% from 35.4% in the previous year largely due to the increase in disbursement for the year amounting to $2.26 billion compared to $1.95 billion in 2018 (Figure 8).[9]

Figure 6: Total Private Sector Portfolio, 2015–2019

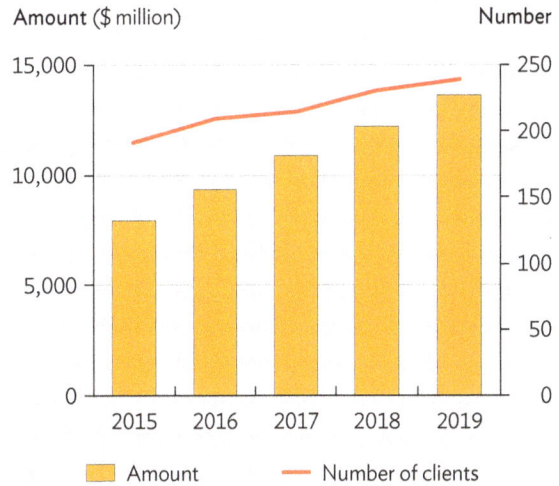

Amount ($ million)   Number

Amount   — Number of clients

Note: Undisbursed programs (Microfinance Risk Participation and Guarantee Program, Supply Chain Finance Program, and Trade Finance Program) not included in 2019.

Source: Asian Development Bank (Private Sector Operations Department).

Figure 7: Total Private Sector Portfolio by Region, 2019 ($ billion)

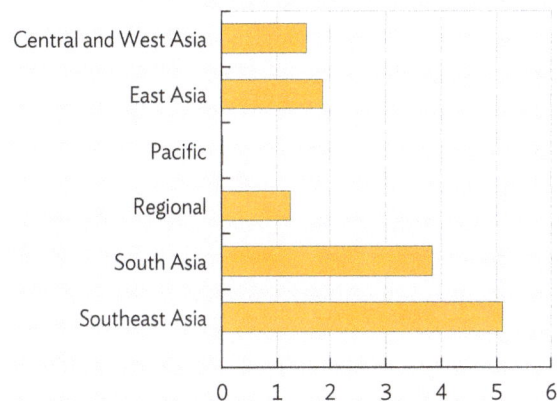

Note: Undisbursed programs (Microfinance Risk Participation and Guarantee Program, Supply Chain Finance Program, and Trade Finance Program) not included.

Source: Asian Development Bank (Private Sector Operations Department).

---

[8]   Frontier countries are low-income and lower-middle-income countries, excluding India; fragile and conflict-affected situations; and small island developing states.

[9]   The disbursement ratio for the year is computed as the amount disbursed during the year divided by the undrawn balance at the beginning of the year, plus signed amounts during the year, less any cancellation.

Figure 8: Private Sector Disbursements, 2015–2019

Amount ($ million) / Ratio (%)

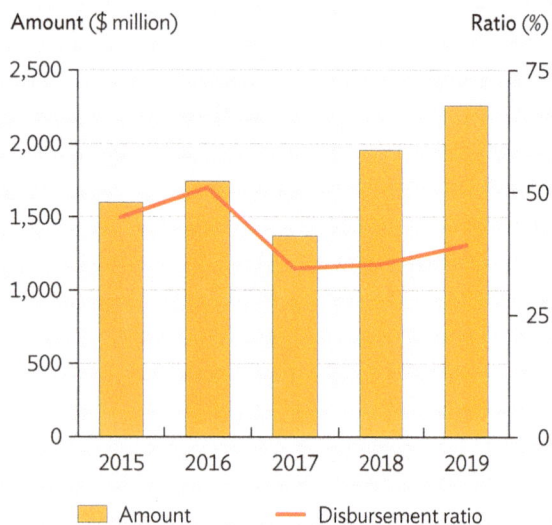

Source: Asian Development Bank (Private Sector Operations Department).

Figure 9: Infrastructure Sector Commitments, 2015–2019

Amount ($ million) / Number

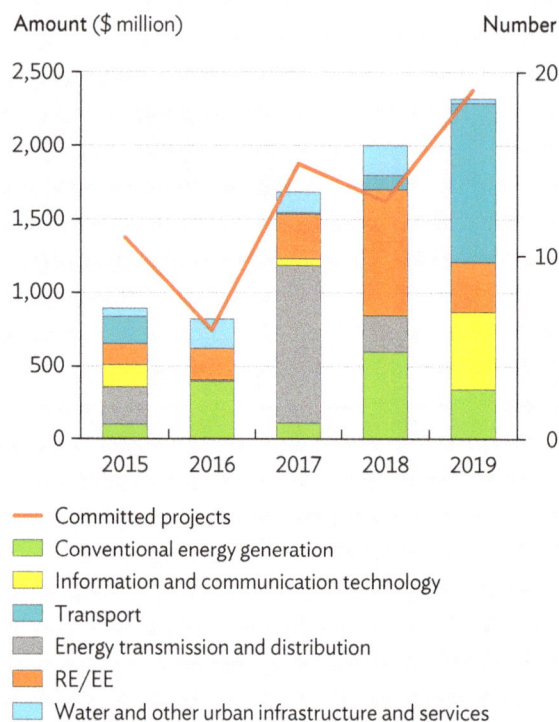

— Committed projects
■ Conventional energy generation
■ Information and communication technology
■ Transport
■ Energy transmission and distribution
■ RE/EE
■ Water and other urban infrastructure and services

RE/EE = renewable energy and/or energy efficiency.
Source: Asian Development Bank (Private Sector Operations Department).

Projects by Sector, 2015–2019

Infrastructure

Infrastructure is widely viewed as a stimulus to economic growth. In the region, however, a significant gap in the supply of long-term financing for infrastructure persists, leading to a massive infrastructure investment requirement. ADB sees the need to mobilize private sector investments to augment the funding gap, a move widely seen as a consensus solution to address the severely lacking infrastructure. To improve living conditions, ADB committed $2.3 billion for 19 new infrastructure projects (Figure 9) in 2019, exceeding the previous record of $2 billion set in 2018. This includes $672 million of climate mitigation financing to promote low-carbon solutions in infrastructure.

In order to expand ADB's private sector operations into underserved markets and challenging infrastructure sectors beyond energy,

PSOD committed $1.1 billion for transport, and $525 million for ICT, the two largest infrastructure subsectors. A transport investment will support the construction of an efficient and reliable mass transport system in Thailand that will move more than 100 million passengers per year. The urban poor, who are most often the victims of long commutes, will largely benefit from this project that will address the increasing demand for reliable transportation. Meanwhile, an ICT investment will help improve access to quality telecommunications services, and increase mobile and broadband penetration rates by expanding access to more than 7 million subscribers in the region. Ensuring the provision of this critical infrastructure will enable better access to information, knowledge, and social and economic opportunities in unserved and underserved areas in less developed DMCs.

Energy remained a valuable sector for ADB where it will continue to focus on delivering green, sustainable, resilient, and inclusive energy infrastructure to sustainably meet the growing demand for energy in the region. In 2019, PSOD expanded its commitments to renewable energy projects, financing 10 more climate-friendly power projects amounting to $346 million. These include funding support for solar, wind, geothermal, hydropower, and WTE projects in 10 countries across the region, and an investment on a green bond project that will be used to finance new renewable energy projects in the Philippines, Indonesia, and Viet Nam. ADB's role as an anchor investor in green bonds will help these instruments and standards be better recognized in the Association of Southeast Asian Nations (ASEAN) capital markets as a compelling alternative to the loan markets for financing clean energy initiatives in the private sector.

Energy generation projects committed in 2019 will add generation capacity of more than 6,715 megawatts (MW), resulting in annual generation of 27,616 gigawatt-hours (GWh) of additional electricity, enough to power over 2.1 million households in the region.

PSOD's infrastructure portfolio has grown to $8.2 billion, based on strong growth in energy projects (Table 2). Infrastructure now accounts for 61% of PSOD's portfolio. Active energy projects have installed 19,518 MW generation capacity and delivered 36,358 GWh of power to DMCs' electricity grids. This power output is enough to serve more than 2.7 million households in the region, of which 37,875 new households have already been provided with reliable access to clean electricity.

Moreover, ADB has scaled up its efforts to advance private sector participation in water infrastructure projects. These investments, however, have been historically concentrated in a limited number of markets due to unattractiveness of the sector in most DMCs for private investments.

Table 2: **Portfolio by Primary Transaction Sector, 2015–2019**

	2015	2016	2017	2018	2019
Infrastructure	4,879	4,871	6,149	6,936	8,235
Clean Energy	2,015	1,906	2,159	2,446	2,798
Conventional Energy	1,798	1,811	2,814	3,302	3,083
Urban and Water	464	542	585	733	512
Transport	431	462	421	327	1,274
ICT	170	150	170	128	568
Finance	2,699	4,034	4,379	4,908	4,849
Agriculture	245	299	260	430	409
Others[a]	126	112	105	205	117
	7,950	**9,316**	**10,893**	**12,479**	**13,610**

ICT = information and communication technology.

[a] "Others" refers to industry and trade, education, and health.

Source: Asian Development Bank (Private Sector Operations Department).

With continuing pressure brought by climate change and rapid rise in population, the water infrastructure sector may find itself under further supply stress without sufficient and sustainable financing. To help resolve the crisis, PSOD continues to engage in water and sanitation projects to crowd in more private sector financing and support the expansion of coverage in the sector. As of 2019, active projects have supplied over 875 million cubic meters of clean and potable water, and treated 1.1 billion cubic meters of wastewater in the region, while connecting more than 769,166 households to a reliable water supply source.

Financial Institutions

Resilient capital markets and financial institutions are vital as well in establishing strong economies. However, in most DMCs, the finance sector remains underdeveloped and characterized by low access to finance largely due to inadequate financing and risk aversion to certain customer segments, among others. ADB's commitments to financial institutions remain diverse.

In 2019, PSOD committed 12 new projects in the finance sector totaling $581 million (Figure 10), of which 4 are private equity funds and 8 are financial institutions. Of the 12 projects committed in 2019, 6 are equity investments while the remaining 6 projects were financed through debt. Through these investments with various financial intermediaries, the finance sector is able to supplement direct interventions in certain socioeconomic areas such as in health and housing, by improving access to health care financing in far-flung areas, and supporting mortgage and home renovation financing for low-income households.

Figure 10: Financial Institution Commitments, 2015–2019

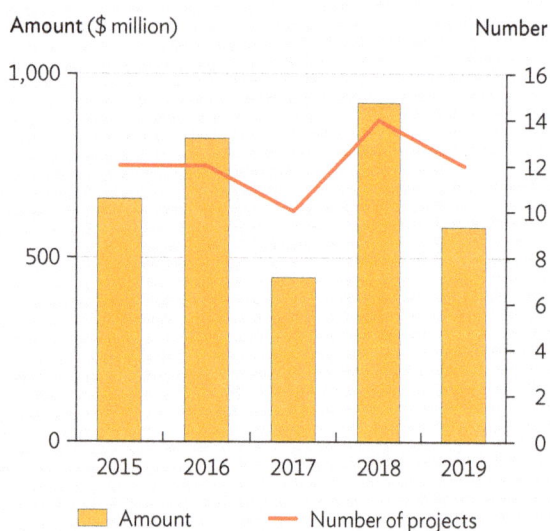

Source: Asian Development Bank (Private Sector Operations Department).

The lack of access to formal finance is a big challenge for many enterprises, hindering their opportunities for business expansion which, in turn, restricts their ability to create new employment opportunities particularly for micro and small enterprises. To address issues in limited credit access, ADB partners with credible financial institutions that have the ability to reach the underserved, in order to turn the tide and deliver profitable results for these underbanked segments. In 2019, most financial institution transactions committed remained focused on financial inclusion of underserved populations, mostly women, microentrepreneurs, and people living in rural areas.

PSOD's financial institution clients are anticipated to provide access to financial services for 2.7 million additional individuals or MSMEs, 2.6 million of whom are expected to be women, or firms owned or operated by women. A total of $5.6 million MSME loans are specifically targeted toward rural customers and agribusinesses. These interventions will provide direct beneficiaries with financial products and services to cover their investment and working capital needs to support growth and expansion.

As shown earlier in Table 2, the portfolio of finance sector projects committed in 2019 amounted to $4.8 billion. A component of these projects aims to reduce gender financing gaps in financial inclusion. Active projects have provided financial services to 24.6 million women and female-owned MSMEs out of approximately 33.2 million total MSME beneficiaries. Increasing the financing available for women and female-owned businesses would contribute in reducing gender financing gaps where, at present, the average loan size of female borrowers is lagging behind loans extended to men in the region. Gender-inclusive financial tools and products support the objective of increasing the participation of women in the finance sector.

Agribusiness

Agribusiness is critical to economic and social development. Agribusiness contributes as much as a third of GDP in most DMCs, as the sector includes not only agricultural production but also manufacturing (e.g., fertilizer production, food processing) and services (e.g., logistics, food retail).

The social importance of agribusiness is reflected in its contribution to livelihood opportunities for smallholder farmers, job creation (particularly for women), and food security.

Given the importance of agribusiness to the region's economic growth and social welfare, ADB committed approximately $79 million in 2019 for five agribusiness projects in Bangladesh, the PRC, Indonesia, Kazakhstan, the Kyrgyz Republic, and Mongolia (Figure 11). PSOD's agribusiness projects support rural livelihoods, for example, by investing in firms that provide employment to rural populations, or that source goods from smallholder farmers (particularly female farmers). Projects also contribute to rural development, better market connectivity, and local agricultural value addition. Transactions committed in 2019 will support the livelihoods of 12,400 farmers.

Figure 11: Agribusiness Commitments, 2015–2019

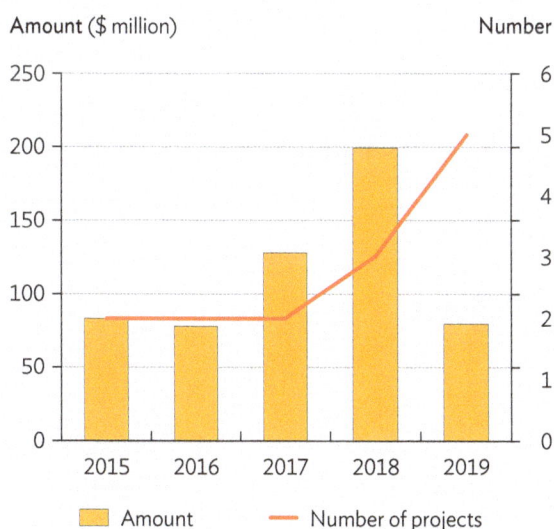

Source: Asian Development Bank (Private Sector Operations Department).

PSOD continues to expand its agribusiness program. At the end of 2019, ADB's PSOD portfolio directly supporting agribusiness financing stood at $409 million. In addition to this, PSOD supports the sector through the financial inclusion of agricultural MSMEs. Active PSOD projects have reached 1.47 million farmers and rural households, which have received financial services or been included in agribusiness value chains.

Social Sectors—Health and Education

Education and health are fundamental to sustainable development. The development benefits of education extend beyond economic growth and include technological advancement, better health choices, improved civic participation, and many others. Similarly, good health allows full economic participation, improves productivity, and reduces poverty. To place greater emphasis on these sectors, PSOD established a social sector team in 2018. ADB will continue to build this team, and PSO activities will focus on improved access to affordable and quality services, employability and job creation, and demonstration of commercial viability of private service delivery models in developing areas such as elderly care and PPPs. As of 2019, 35,568 students have been reached by the current portfolio, and 8.8 million patients have been served.

In 2019, PSOD committed approximately $19 million for a tertiary education project in Southeast Asia, a hospital bond project in Georgia, and an equity investment with Kaizen Equity II Private Limited. Approximately 50,000 students are expected to be reached and 14,350 patients to be served from the commitments in 2019.

CATALYZING AND MOBILIZING COFINANCING

▲ **250-megawatt power plant.** The Tianjin Integrated Gasification Combined Cycle Power Plant Project is in the Tianjin Harbor Industrial Park in the Binhai New Area of Tianjin City (photo by ADB).

ADB mobilized long-term cofinancing of $3.54 billion in 2019, with more than 90% coming from commercial cofinancing partners, and the rest from official sources. This cofinancing was against ADB's own financing commitment of $2.35 billion, net of risk transfers. In effect, every $1.00 of ADB's own funds was matched by $1.50 in long-term cofinancing. Out of the 38 nonsovereign projects signed in 2019, 19 featured cofinancing from partners.

ADB's Strategy 2030 sets a cofinancing target ratio of 2.5. In 2018, the ratio was 1.2, and steady progress toward the goal is underway.

One of the cofinancing projects signed in 2019 is in Indonesia, where communities will gain access to more affordable and reliable electricity through a 275 MW combined-cycle gas turbine power plant constructed in Riau province, central Sumatra.

The power plant will help secure Indonesia's energy future by generating 1,445 GWh of electricity per year and reduce carbon emissions by 375,000 tons per year by 2022. This financing package consists of the following:

(i) $70 million loan from ADB;
(ii) $82 million B-loan from Sumitomo Mitsui Banking Corporation and MUFG Bank, with ADB providing a partial risk guarantee to the participating commercial banks; and
(iii) $20 million loan administration from the Leading Asia's Private Sector Infrastructure Fund (LEAP).

The power plant will be implemented by P.T. Medco Ratch Power Riau, a special purpose vehicle partially owned by P.T. Medco Power Indonesia, a leading developer and operator of small and medium-sized independent power producers in the country; and Ratchaburi Electricity Generating Holding Public Company Limited, Thailand's largest independent power producer.

In Thailand, the financing package for a power plant consists of the following:

(i) $50 million direct loan;
(ii) $85 million in B-loan;
(iii) $45 million through the LEAP;
(iv) $208 million from the Japan Bank of International Cooperation; and
(v) $764 million in commercial cofinancing.

The 2,500 MW, combined-cycle, gas turbine power plant in the Rojana Rayong 2 Industrial Park, Rayong Province, is to be built and operated by Gulf PD Company Limited.

In Pakistan, Kashf Foundation, a not-for-profit microfinance institution, will expand its lending operations by providing the following financing package:

(i) $15 million from ADB's own resources;
(ii) $5 million from the Netherlands Development Finance Company to extend the B-loan; and
(iii) $5 million from the Swiss impact fund, responsAbility Investments AG.

This is the first time responsAbility Investments AG, a key international impact investor, is participating in an ADB-financed project. Facilitating the participation of responsAbility Investments AG is representative of ADB's efforts to expand the universe of cofinancing partners.

CONTRIBUTIONS TO STRATEGY 2030 OPERATIONAL PRIORITIES

▶ **Solar driers for apricot farmers in Pakistan.** ADB supports Kashf Foundation's lending to low-income women, and female micro and small entrepreneurs in Pakistan (photo by ADB).

Strategy 2030 defines the operational priorities to achieve ADB's vision of a prosperous, inclusive, resilient, and sustainable Asia and the Pacific. Given the critical role the private sector plays as a key contributor to economic growth in developing economies, ADB is committed to expanding its private sector operations to reach one-third of total operations in number by 2024. To achieve this objective, ADB will expand into new and frontier markets, scaling up operations beyond traditional infrastructure and finance sectors in such segments as environmental infrastructure, transport, ICT, agribusiness, and education and health. ADB will enhance its local currency offerings and further develop its equity investments platform while mobilizing more cofinancing through its credit enhancement, syndications, and asset management activities in line with its mobilization targets of $2.50 of long-term cofinancing for every $1.00 in own financing.

While the future of Asia and the Pacific depends upon a dynamic private sector, significant challenges in business environments and gaps in financial markets continue to prevent the region from realizing more inclusive and sustainable growth. In some parts of Asia, these challenges and gaps are massive. Developing Asia alone will require annual infrastructure investments of $1.7 trillion (or $26 trillion from 2016 to 2030). A notable 30% of the $1.5 trillion global trade finance gap originates from developing Asia.

Asian capital markets, especially in developing Asia, lag most of the world, and specialized, important financial products such as project bonds and climate bonds remain underdeveloped. The lack of long-term local currency financing impedes investment and reinforces a real gap in further growth and/or creates potential foreign exchange imbalances.

ADB is best suited to respond to and tackle these gaps and challenges by leveraging its sovereign and nonsovereign operations. For sovereign operations, policy advice, technical assistance, policy-based lending, and project lending help DMCs foster enabling market conditions and the institutional capacity required to attract private sector investment. Through its nonsovereign operations, ADB can help raise environmental, social, and governance standards; provide financing that may not be available from the market (either at all or on reasonable terms); improve project design and development outcomes; and mitigate perceived risks to design, accelerate, and achieve meaningful development results.

1. Addressing Remaining Poverty and Reducing Inequalities

In 2019, ADB's private sector operations continued to assist DMCs in broadening access to financial services to support health care and education. ADB focused 21% of its private sector operations on inclusive business initiatives that provide economic opportunities to the poor.

In 2019, PSOD signed agreements for eight inclusive business transactions (Figure 12).

Figure 12: **Inclusive Business Projects Committed, 2015–2019**

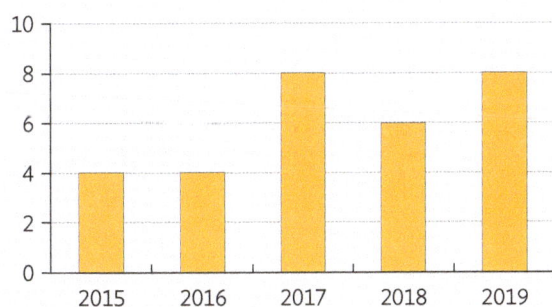

Source: Asian Development Bank (Private Sector Operations Department).

Most of these transactions focus on providing financial services to the underserved (Box 2), on improving rural livelihoods, or on providing health services to underprivileged segments of the population.

In the PRC, Far East Horizon Limited, one of the PRC's leading financial services groups, received a $150 million loan from ADB to provide lease financing to public hospitals in 12 least developed provinces, where the per capita income is the lowest among the 31 provinces of the PRC. Majority of the rural population will directly benefit from the project, which will reduce the need for long-distance travel to city hospitals as county hospital facilities are upgraded. Far East Horizon, which has over 20 years of experience in health care leasing, is expected to finance the lease or purchase of modern medical equipment; and the construction, expansion, or refurbishment of hospital buildings and associated medical facilities of 50 public hospitals. Also, the project is expected to reduce the regional disparity in health care standards, widen access to quality health care, and improve delivery of health services in rural areas. At present, local areas are significantly underserved by the health care system where average health care expenditure is only 40% of the level in urban areas.

In Southeast Asia, ADB invested a combined $12.5 million from its own fund and the Leading Asia's Private Sector Infrastructure Fund (LEAP) to support PHINMA Education Holdings' plan for capacity expansion and acquisition of new tertiary education institutions. PHINMA will improve access to quality tertiary education and increase employability, especially for students from low-income households in both countries. The project will focus on students from low-income households, to improve their access to quality tertiary education and increase their employability. PHINMA is expected to expand student enrollment from 68,819 to 114,000 during its first 5 years of operation.

Box 2

India—Inclusive Business Finance and Gender Project in Lagging States

Fullerton India Credit Company Limited extends financing to micro, small, and medium-sized enterprises (MSMEs). The Asian Development Bank (ADB) loaned $150 million to Fullerton so it can expand its lending particularly to borrowers in lagging areas, as well as women-led MSMEs. Fullerton aims to reach at least 2.9 million MSME borrowers, including 2.67 million women; and 950,000 MSME borrowers from underserved states.

▲ **MSME support.** ADB's loan to Fullerton will make loans accessible particularly to women entrepreneurs (photo by ADB).

Source: Asian Development Bank (Private Sector Operations Department).

In 2019, ADB ventured into its first satellite financing to provide wide access to broadband internet connections in remote areas in Asia and the Pacific, where internet coverage is limited or not available. Access to broadband internet connections can stimulate economic growth and generate employment, thereby reducing poverty and inequality between rural and urban areas, and between developed and developing countries.

ADB provided a $50 million financing package to Kacific Broadband Satellites International Limited to support the construction, launch, and operation of a shared, geostationary earth orbit, high-throughput satellite featuring Ka-band technology (Kacific-1). The satellite was successfully launched on 7 December 2019 from Cape Canaveral, Florida, and will have a minimum useful life of 15 years. It is expected to operate for 20–25 years.

This project demonstrates how ADB can contribute to the extensive use of technology and innovation by expanding internet access in Asia and the Pacific.

2. Accelerating Progress in Gender Equality

PSOD works with clients to enhance gender equity by supporting projects designed to benefit women. In 2019, PSOD committed 31 projects with gender elements to help women improve their livelihoods, or make the work environment more supportive of women and their needs (Figure 13).

Figure 13: Commitments with Gender Elements, 2015–2019

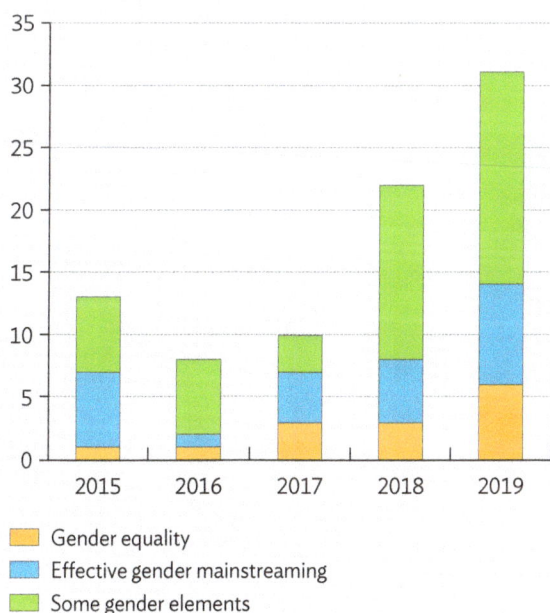

Gender equality
Effective gender mainstreaming
Some gender elements

Source: Asian Development Bank (Private Sector Operations Department).

Eight of the 31 projects deliver outcomes that directly support gender equality and women's empowerment by narrowing gender disparities. In Pakistan, ADB provided a $25 million loan to assist Kashf Foundation, one of the country's leading microfinance service providers, to support lending operations to low-income households and women-led MSMEs.

Through Kashf, women will be empowered economically through quality and cost-effective microfinance services, and greater access to finance.

In Mongolia, ADB provided a $30 million loan to XacBank, the country's fourth largest commercial bank, to support its lending operations to MSMEs, including those led by women and located outside Ulaanbataar. Through its gender action plan, XacBank will incorporate measures to promote gender equality and/or women empowerment in its business activities; enhance its outreach campaigns targeting 1,000 women-led MSMEs; strengthen staff skills on gender sensitization and respectful work environment; and establish a comprehensive program to heighten awareness and support to women borrowers. The improved access to finance will support the expansion of MSMEs and diversification of the economy, which in turn will contribute to employment and poverty reduction. This is the second ADB loan to XacBank; however, this is the first time that ADB's loan may be partially denominated in the local currency (*togrog*).

In Myanmar, ADB committed a $500 million loan to support the rolling out of fixed and wireless broadband services and upgrading of Ooredoo QPSC's mobile telecommunications networks. The initiative will improve people's access to quality telecommunication services that will enable better access to information, knowledge, and social and economic opportunities. In particular, the investment aims to reduce digital gender gaps by increasing women's basic access to ICT and by facilitating the provision of ICT jobs, promotion, training, and health services for women. The investment will help Ooredoo increase its active subscribers to 15 million by 2023 of which almost 50% are expected to be women.

Box 3 illustrates how ADB-supported projects promoted gender equality in the Philippines and Georgia.

Box 3
Georgia and the Philippines—Support to Women Entrepreneurs and Borrowers

ASA Philippines Foundation

The ASA Philippines Foundation is a microfinance nongovernment organization that provides financing solely to low-income women borrowers to meet their livelihood and business needs. The foundation is a recipient of a $30 million loan from the Asian Development Bank (ADB) meant to broaden access to finance for women-owned microenterprises especially in conflict-impacted and lagging areas. The foundation will expand its portfolio of business loans to microenterprises and strengthen its resource base for providing loans to micro-housing, water supply, and on-site sanitation for women borrowers. This will improve women's income levels, savings, and overall living conditions. The project aims to expand its outreach to at least 2 million women borrowers across the country by 2024.

▲ **Textile business owned by a woman in Mindanao.** ADB's loan to ASA helps improve access to finance for low-income women borrowers to meet their livelihood and business needs (photo by ASA Philippines Foundation, Inc.).

Credo Bank, Georgia

In Georgia, Credo Bank will launch new products including home improvement and mortgage loans to lower-income households in rural areas and those located at the periphery of the country's capital, Tbilisi. Credo Bank will expand its services to small business and rural household customers, most of whom are women. The bank also aims to provide mortgage and home renovation loans to at least 26,000 borrowers by 2023, half of which will be female borrowers. These will all be facilitated by a $22.3 million loan and $500,000 technical assistance grant from ADB.

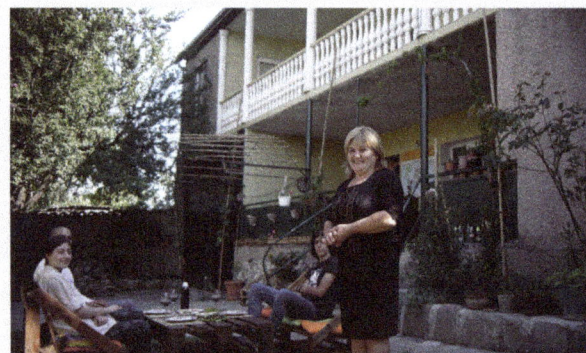

▲ **Home construction and renovation financing.** Low-income residents, particularly women in rural Georgia and outside the capital, are serviced by Credo Bank (photo by ADB).

Source: Asian Development Bank (Private Sector Operations Department).

3. Tackling Climate Change, Building Climate and Disaster Resilience, and Enhancing Environmental Sustainability

ADB continues to play a major role in financing climate-related projects in Asia and the Pacific, largely through its infrastructure focus. It also provides climate-related financing through financial institutions. In 2019, PSOD committed $722 million to climate financing (Figure 14), which is expected to result in investments that will reduce greenhouse gas emissions by 7.64 million tons of carbon dioxide equivalent (tCO_2e). PSOD's active portfolio contributes to emission reductions of 30.66 million tCO_2e per year as of 2019.

Figure 14: Committed Climate Funding, 2017–2019
($ million)

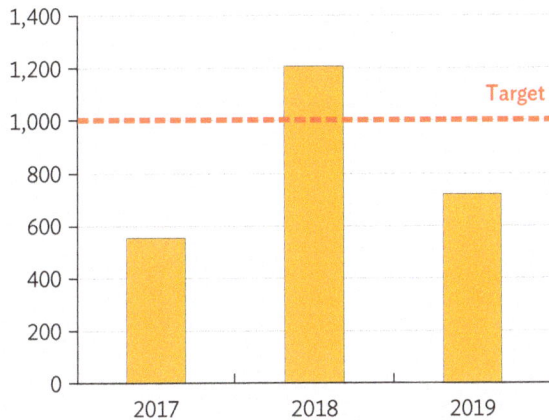

Source: Asian Development Bank (Private Sector Operations Department).

In Armenia, a 250 MW, gas-fired, combined-cycle cogeneration power plant is being constructed and will be operated by ArmPower CJSC—the country's first greenfield project-financed power plant. The plant will have an annual generation capacity of 1,981 GWh. Through a $44 million loan support from ADB, the project will contribute to the diversification of energy sources in the country, and boost efficiency and reliability by helping to replace aging power generation assets with modern facilities.

In Kazakhstan, a 135 MW solar plant is intended to ease power supply shortages and boost the share of renewable source in the country's energy mix. This will be one of the largest solar power projects in Central and West Asia. It constitutes an important step to support the country's plan to transition to a green economy and boost the share of clean energy to 50% of total power generation by 2050. Using a $29.75 million loan commitment from ADB, M-KAT Green LLP will construct and operate the plant, which is proposed to generate about 207 GWh of electricity annually and reduce 120,500 tCO_2e annually. ADB is also assisting Baikonyr Solar LLP in Kazakhstan with an $11.5 million loan to further enhance the country's

energy security through increased solar renewable sources. The project includes construction and operation of a 50 MW solar power plant, which is expected to generate 73 GWh of electricity and reduce 40,800 tCO_2e per year.

In India, ADB committed a combined $50 million investment from its own fund and LEAP to Avaada Energy Private Limited to help the company expand solar photovoltaic generation capacity in the country to 1,991 MW by 2023. The project will help increase the share of renewable energy in the country's generation capacity, and help reduce India's emission intensity. The project is expected to generate 4,400 GWh of electricity, and reduce 3.86 million tCO_2e annually starting 2024. It also aims to create more than 333 new jobs during the plant's operation.

In Nepal, a 216 MW run-of-river hydropower plant will be constructed on the Trishuli River. Once operational, the plant is expected to provide over 1,200 GWh of clean electricity to the grid and reduce 446,000 tCO_2e annually. The project will enhance Nepal's energy security by helping to utilize its renewable hydropower resources and reduce imports of electricity. ADB committed a $60 million loan—comprising $30 million from its own resources and $30 million by way of administration of a loan from the Canadian Climate Fund for the Private Sector in Asia II—to Nepal Water and Energy Development Company Private Limited, which will build and operate the plant. The project is one of the largest private sector investments in Nepal to date.

In Mongolia, ADB financed its first private sector solar power project. A combined loan support of $18.7 million loan from ADB's own fund and LEAP to Sermsang Power Corporation Public Company Limited and Tenuun Gerel Construction LLC will build and operate a 15 MW solar power plant in the country. The plant is expected to generate clean electricity totaling 22.3 GWh annually, and reduce carbon dioxide emissions by 26,400 tons per year.

Box 4
Viet Nam—ADB's First Floating Solar Panels Project

In Viet Nam, the Da Nhim–Ham Thuan–Da Mi Hydro Power Joint Stock Company received a $37 million loan from the Asian Development Bank (ADB) to finance the installation of a 47.5-megawatt floating solar photovoltaic power facility on the man-made reservoir of the company's existing 175-megawatt Da Mi hydropower plant.

The project marks the first large-scale installation of floating solar panels in Viet Nam and is the largest installation in Southeast Asia. It will help boost the share of renewable energy in the country's energy mix and decrease the dependence on coal for energy generation. The project aims to generate at least 63,000 megawatt-hours of electricity and reduce at least 30,000 tons of carbon dioxide by 2023.

The loan package consists of $17.6 million from ADB's own fund, supplemented with $15 million from the Canadian Climate Fund for the Private Sector in Asia I and II; and $4.4 million from the Leading Asia's Private Sector Infrastructure Fund, both of which are administered by ADB.

▲ **View over the floating solar photovoltaic power generation panels at the Da Mi hydro power plant in Viet Nam.** The Floating Solar Energy Project of the Da Nhim–Ham Thuan–Da Mi Hydro Power Joint Stock Company will install floating solar photovoltaic power generation panels on the man-made reservoir of its existing 175-megawatt Da Mi hydropower plant (photo by Gerhard Joren for ADB).

Source: Asian Development Bank (Private Sector Operations Department).

It will help the government increase the share of renewable energy in total installed capacity, and lessen the country's dependence on coal for electricity generation.

2019 likewise saw ADB's first floating solar panels project (Box 4).

4. Making Cities More Livable

In 2019, ADB private sector operations also provided solutions to help build cities that are more livable, affordable, and sustainable. This included WTE projects, wastewater treatment, and transportation.

In the PRC, Shanghai SUS Environment Company Limited will finance a portfolio of innovative WTE facilities within low carbon eco-industrial parks through a $100 million ADB loan. The investment will expand the PRC's low-carbon circular economy and make cities more livable through an integrated urban waste management system. The WTE facilities will treat 1.1 million tons of municipal solid waste, generate 275 GWh of clean energy, and reduce carbon dioxide equivalent emissions by about 737,154 million tons annually. This project marks ADB's first eco-industrial park WTE project.

Also in the PRC, ADB committed a $60.75 million loan to Maxwealth Financial Leasing Company Limited to support its lease finance operations to wastewater treatment plants for industrial and municipal wastewater treatment in the country. Maxwealth Financial Leasing Company Limited will extend lease financing to at least six wastewater treatment plants. The project will help increase wastewater treatment capacity in the country, and improve the urban environment and quality of life for residents. A total of 2.2 million people are expected to benefit from the improved wastewater treatment services.

In transportation, ADB committed $311 million for the construction of the Pink and Yellow lines of Bangkok's mass rapid system; and $746.21 million to support the Indian Railway Finance Corporation improve existing railways lines in India, its largest single nonsovereign loan ever committed (Box 5).

5. Promoting Rural Development and Food Security

In 2019, ADB continued to promote rural development and food security through its agribusiness operations, which support climate-smart agriculture and food processors and distributors that embrace inclusive and environmentally responsible business practices.

RG Brands is modernizing production infrastructure through an ADB loan of $12.5 million to strengthen the company's regional distribution chain. The loan will finance the purchase of 18,750 energy-efficient coolers for small convenience stores on RG Brands' distribution chain in Kazakhstan and the Kyrgyz Republic, at least half of which will be owned by women. Modernization of the company's production facilities will help to reduce costs and improve energy efficiency, while the coolers will help reduce carbon dioxide emissions by 4,200 tons. Shopkeepers should see their livelihoods improved, and women empowerment would be more strongly supported in Kazakhstan and the Kyrgyz Republic through this assistance, which is ADB's second loan to RG Brands.

Meanwhile, the coconut agro-industry in Indonesia is receiving a boost through a $5 million loan support from ADB to PT SASL and Sons Indonesia for development of the coconut agro-industry in Central Sulawesi. PT SASL and Sons Indonesia will put up a modern processing plant to manufacture high-value coconut products for export. At full operational capacity, the new processing plant is expected to produce over 9,400 metric tons per year of desiccated coconut and 2,500 metric tons of virgin coconut oil. The plant will benefit about 9,500 smallholder coconut farmers and create jobs for more than 1,200 people in Central Sulawesi, mostly women.

In the PRC, a business model for livestock production that is inclusive, resource-efficient, and has lower environmental impacts will be adopted by New Hope Liuhe Co. Ltd. The model will help expand the company's integrated livestock business with the construction of two hog farms and a meat-processing facility. Installation of biogas digesters within the hog farms will ensure effective waste management and help reduce carbon dioxide emissions by at least 8,000 tons per year. The company, which is benefiting from a $40 million loan from ADB, will integrate 1,000 smallholder farmers into the company's hog production value chain.

Box 5
Thailand—Pink and Yellow Mass Rapid Transport Lines, and India—Railways Lines

Pink and Yellow Mass Rapid Transport Lines, Thailand

Two new lines in Thailand will generate 2,000 jobs and are expected to run a combined 592,000 passenger trips per day upon its operation by 2030. The Asian Development Bank (ADB) committed a $311 million loan for the construction of the Pink and Yellow lines of Bangkok's mass rapid transit system. The Pink Line, to be operated by Northern Bangkok Monorail Company Limited, will have a total length of 34.5 kilometers running between Min Buri District in Bangkok and Khae Rai in Nonthaburi Province. The Yellow Line, to be operated by the Eastern Bangkok Monorail Company Limited, will run from Lat Phrao in Bangkok to Samrong in Samut Prakan Province, with a total length of about 30 kilometers.

Railways Lines, India

India's rail system relies heavily on fossil fuels. In a route that crosses 13 states in the country consisting of approximately 3,378 kilometers of railway tracks, electric traction will replace diesel-powered trains through a $746.21 million ADB loan to Indian Railway Finance Corporation. The investment is the largest single nonsovereign loan ever committed by ADB aimed to improve existing railways lines. The project will be critical for the movement of goods and people within the country. Migrating passenger and freight traffic from diesel to electric traction is more advantageous since it is inexpensive to operate, uses renewable energy, and recovers energy from braking or slowing down of the train.

▲ **Mass rapid transit monorail lines.** Two mass rapid transit monorail lines, Pink Line and Yellow Line, will operate in Bangkok; and in Nonthaburi and Sumut Prakarn provinces (photo by BTS).

▲ **Electrification of railways.** ADB is supporting the electrification of approximately 3,378 kilometers of existing railway tracks traversing 13 states in India (photo by ADB).

Source: Asian Development Bank (Private Sector Operations Department).

Box 6
Bangladesh and Mongolia—Agribusiness Financing

Sylvan Agriculture Limited, Bangladesh

Sylvan Agriculture Limited (SAL), part of the PRAN group, is one of the largest foods and agribusiness companies in Bangladesh. Through a $14.2 million loan from the Asian Development Bank (ADB), SAL will finance new food processing facilities to produce potato-based products and pasta. The project will integrate 2,000 contract farmers who will supply quality potatoes for the new processing facilities. The farmers shall be growing new potato varieties that will increase their income by at least 50%. This project is ADB's first repeat private sector assistance to an agribusiness company and will expand the area the farmers cultivate, with the added assurance that their production will be bought by SAL.

▲ **A woman potato farmer supplying the PRAN group.** With an ADB loan in place, Sylvan Agriculture Limited intends to procure potatoes under contract farming arrangements and provide secure income to 2,000 smallholder farmers (photo by ADB).

Milko, Mongolia

In Mongolia, ADB will assist Milko as it expands its raw milk and fruit procurement and dairy processing capacity. The increased raw milk and fruit procurement capacity will benefit around 1,000 smallholder farmers and herders, most of whom are women. Gender equality will be promoted at all stages of the dairy value chain, including increasing the share of direct payments made to women farmer's bank accounts, and the proportion of women in Milko's staff and board of directors will likewise be increased. Pregnant and lactating mothers will also benefit from the production of micronutrient-fortified dairy products. Additionally, ADB's $7.4 million equivalent local currency loan will help Milko increase exports of its end-products.

▲ **A female dairy farmer supplying Milko.** Milko's dairy-processing capacity and its raw milk and fruit procurement capacity have been increased through an ADB loan (photo by Milko LLC).

Source: Asian Development Bank (Private Sector Operations Department).

In 2019, ADB committed $14.2 million in direct agribusiness financing to support Sylvan Agriculture Limited in Bangladesh, one of the largest food processing facilities in the country; and to Milko in Mongolia, to help expand its raw milk and fruit procurement and dairy processing capacity (Box 6).

6. Strengthening Governance and Institutional Capacity

ADB helps strengthen the business environment for private sector development. Box 7 summarizes some activities of PSOD in 2019 that would help SMEs pursue good governance and improve access to capital and performance.

Box 7
Technical Assistance for Governance

Corporate Governance Training

Experts from the International Financial Corporation's Corporate Governance Group conducted a 2-day training course for deal teams from the Private Sector Operations Department (PSOD) on applying development finance institution corporate governance toolkits as part of initial project due diligence. Case studies on implementing and monitoring action plans were presented.

2019 Annual DFI Corporate Governance Conference

PSOD attended the 13th Annual DFI Corporate Governance Conference in Washington, DC in March 2019. The annual conference provides a forum for the Asian Development Bank (ADB) and other development finance institutions to find solutions to common problems in implementing corporate governance in developing countries.

Asia Corporate Governance Association Annual Members Conference

PSOD participated in the 2018 Annual Congress of the Asia Corporate Governance Association in Beijing. PSOD is an active member of the association, which is committed to lobbying governments and industry groups to adopt good corporate governance policies and legislation throughout the Asia and Pacific region.

Source: Asian Development Bank (Private Sector Operations Department).

7. Fostering Regional Cooperation and Integration

ADB supports regional cooperation and integration by financing cross-border infrastructure projects and investments in companies that transfer technology and best practices in DMCs. In 2019, PSOD committed seven regional cooperation and integration projects for $129 million (Figure 15).

In 2019, ADB committed $50 million as an additional capital contribution to support continuous guarantee operations of the Credit Guarantee Investment Facility. The facility was created by ADB as a trust fund to help develop local currency and regional bond markets in the ASEAN+3 region.[10]

Figure 15: Regional Cooperation and Integration Projects Committed, 2015–2019

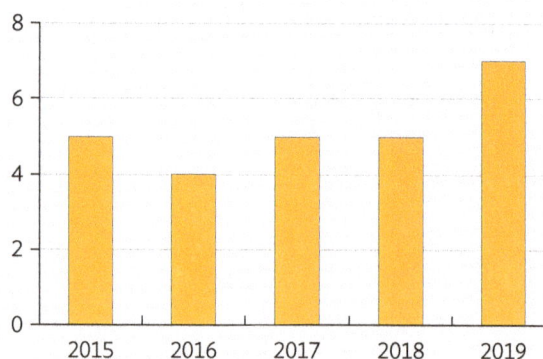

Source: Asian Development Bank (Private Sector Operations Department).

---

[10] The ASEAN+3 region is composed of Brunei Darussalam, Cambodia, the People's Republic of China, Indonesia, Japan, the Republic of Korea, the Lao People's Democratic Republic, Malaysia, Myanmar, the Philippines, Thailand, and Viet Nam.

The infusion will support regional cooperation and promote financial resilience by allowing corporations and infrastructure projects to gain access to local currency and regional bond markets.

ADB also committed $20 million in the maiden climate bond issuance of AC Energy Finance International Limited, a wholly owned subsidiary of Ayala Corporation in the Philippines, to promote financing of clean energy projects by the private sector across the region. The proceeds of the bond will be used to finance solar and wind energy projects in Indonesia, the Philippines, and Viet Nam. This is ADB's first publicly listed climate bond and third climate bond project. This regional project will support private sector financing of green energy options across Southeast Asia.

Since its inception in 2009, ADB's Trade Finance Program (TFP) has been helping close market gaps for trade finance. For 2019, the program facilitated 4,832 transactions valued at $5.4 billion, with $3.5 billion cofinanced by banks, private insurers, and official agencies. Figure 16 shows TFP's 5-year growth in business and development.

Of the total transactions, 4,069 supported SMEs; 1,361 supported trade between DMCs; while interregional trade was 3,731 (Figure 17). Among the 21 countries covered by the TFP, the most active were Armenia, Bangladesh, Pakistan, Sri Lanka, and Viet Nam.

In 2019, ADB continued to implement its Supply Chain Finance Program (SCFP). For 2019, the program supported 577 transactions valued at $118.7 million, with $59.3 million, or 50%, cofinanced by partner financial institutions. For 2019, 78% of the transactions supported SMEs.

Figure 16: Value of Number of Transactions Supported by the Trade Finance Program, Cofinancing, and Commitments, 2015–2019

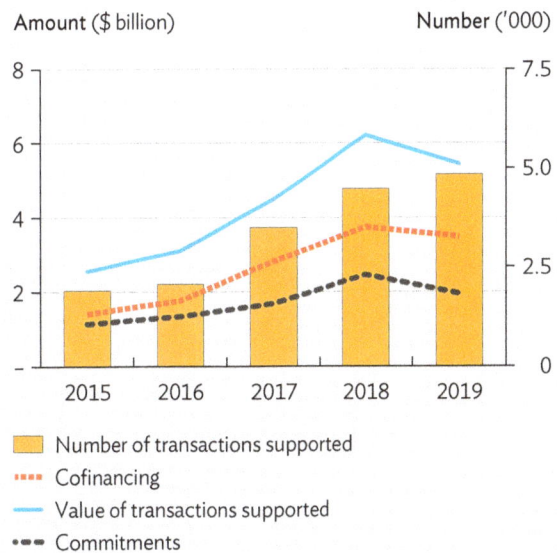

Notes: Value of transactions supported, i.e., the sum of cofinancing and commitments, pertains to the value of underlying trade transactions facilitated through the Trade Finance Program. Commitments pertain to guaranteed and/or disbursed amounts of exposure retained by the Asian Development Bank that are not cofinanced.

Source: Asian Development Bank (Private Sector Operations Department).

Figure 17: Trade Finance Program Transactions Supported, 2015–2019

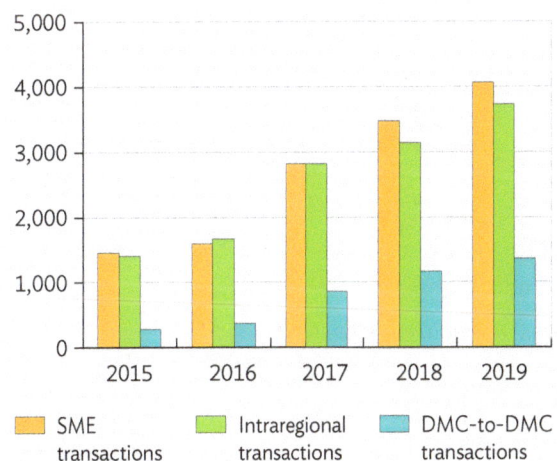

DMC = developing member country, SMEs = small and medium-sized enterprises.

Source: Asian Development Bank (Private Sector Operations Department).

OTHER APPROACHES TO DEVELOPING THE PRIVATE SECTOR

▲ **Pagudpud wind farm in the Philippines.** AC Energy will support private sector financing of green energy options across Southeast Asia (photo by AC Energy).

Widening Geographic Coverage

ADB continues to significantly expand its private sector operations in new and frontier markets including fragile and conflict-affected situations (FCAS) and small island development states.

In the Pacific, power utilities operated by the private sector currently rely on sovereign guarantees to backstop their offtake obligations. However, many governments in the Pacific DMCs cannot provide guarantees due to sovereign debt ceilings, or their preference to access direct borrowing.

With these constraints, the Pacific Renewable Energy Program (PREP) was designed as an umbrella facility to encourage private sector investment. In 2019, ADB approved $100 million for PREP, which uses a blend of financing support and credit enhancement to surmount the current barriers to private investment in the region. ADB sources grant funds for PREP from among its development partners as a credit enhancement tool for Pacific DMCs. Donor funds backstop a 2-year letter of credit to make power payments and mitigate short-term liquidity risk of the power utilities. This is combined with a partial risk guarantee to address long-term liquidity risk and breach of contract, in the event of termination of a power purchase agreement. All these should induce self-sustaining private sector development, reduce continued reliance of power utilities on grants and subsidies, and increase energy supply.

New Zealand's Ministry of Foreign Affairs and Trade is the first donor to support PREP with grant funds. PREP will (i) lower the cost of financing and encourage financing with longer tenors, which will feed through to lower power tariffs; (ii) attract new investors and lenders to the Pacific DMCs, where they might not otherwise invest; and (iii) increase PSOD's focus on frontier markets in accordance with ADB's Strategy 2030.

In Afghanistan—a country classified as FCAS— 77 Construction, Contracting, and Trading Group became the country's first private sector-financed independent power producer through ADB. It will build a 15.1 MW solar power plant with ADB's $4 million loan, which will promote development of renewable energy in the country. The project will generate about 27.5 GWh of electricity and avoid 8,500 tCO_2e annually. As part of the project, ADB will also administer a $3.85 million loan from the Canadian Climate Fund for the Private Sector in Asia II.

Private Equity Funds to Extend Reach

Private sector companies (including small and medium business enterprises) in several sectors such as infrastructure, financial services, renewable energy, health care, education, and agribusiness are growing from ADB's private equity fund investments. These investments aim to drive economic growth and employment, mobilize growth capital to foster development impact, promote good corporate governance, elevate environmental and social practices and compliance, and encourage gender-lens investing.

Private equity fund investments accomplish the following:

(i) they leverage on ADB's geographic presence and local knowledge of fund managers to broaden access to underpenetrated markets and sectors;
(ii) they diversify risk across companies, industries, and regions thereby broadening impact and providing more reliable equity returns; and
(iii) they complement and enhance ADB's direct equity business by partnering with funds that can provide attractive co-investment opportunities.

Since its first private equity fund investment in 1984, ADB has invested over $1.8 billion and mobilized $12 billion of third-party capital into more than 80 private equity funds in DMCs. This includes a $5 million equity investment made in 2019 in Kaizen Private Equity II Private Limited, a $79 million education-focused private equity fund. Improved access to, quality, and affordability of education in lower-middle market segments in South Asia and Southeast Asia are expected to result as Kaizen invests in K-12 education, preschools, online education, vocational training, and test preparation. Additionally, ADB's involvement is expected to help Kaizen garner the trust of institutional financiers and enhance funding availability for the private education sector.

In India, Tata Capital will invest equity capital for minority stakes in a portfolio of 10–12 lower middle-market Indian companies, including SMEs, using proceeds of ADB's $10 million equity investment in Tata Capital Growth Fund II. ADB's equity will focus on, among others, financial services, health care, manufacturing, and information technology. By infusing critical growth capital to well-managed companies operating in sectors that are benefiting from the country's increasing domestic consumption and urbanization, economic development should be spurred.

In the PRC, CDH VGC Fund, L.P. will provide growth capital to about 20 private companies engaged in health care, supply chain and/or consumer, and artificial intelligence and technology using ADB's $30 million equity investment. This capital will help increase the depth and diversity of venture and growth capital business models, encourage entrepreneurship, and support the transition of the PRC economy from one focused on manufacturing, to one driven increasingly by technology and innovation.

In the same manner, growth capital will also be accessible to middle-market companies in the health care, business services, and consumer sectors in the PRC, India, and Southeast Asia through Everbridge Partners Fund I, a targeted private equity fund where ADB also made a $40 million equity investment. Everbridge Partners Fund I will help deepen capital markets and support Asia's growing private sector.

Strengthening the Finance Sector and Capital Markets

In 2019, two bond issuers issued their maiden green bonds: AC Energy Green Bond Project, and Energy Absolute Green Bond for Wind Power Project. AC Energy will support private sector financing of green energy options across Southeast Asia. The Energy Absolute Green Bond was the first green bond for wind power in Thailand, with a total issuance of 10 billion Thai baht.[11]

Through ADB's encouragement, AC Energy obtained the higher "Climate Bond Standard Certified" status to make the offering the first publicly listed climate bond in Southeast Asia (listed on the Singapore Stock Exchange). This regional project will contribute to the objective of ASEAN to source 23% of its primary energy from renewable sources by 2025.

The Energy Absolute Green Bond will support long-term financing of Energy Absolute's 260 MW Hanuman wind farm located in Chaiyaphum Province. This was the first green bond for wind power in Thailand. The project is expected to generate 450 GWh of electricity annually, and reduce Thailand's carbon emissions by 200,000 tons annually.

In Georgia, ADB invested $6.8 million into JSC Evex Hospital's corporate bond issuance. The proceeds of the issuance will be used to refinance some of the hospital's debt and assist it in achieving better operational efficiency, quality of services, and governance. In turn, JSC Evex Hospital can pursue Georgia's universal health care program by serving at least 800,000 patients by 2024. The investment will help in Georgia's capital market development, particularly the deepening of its corporate debt securities and overall local currency bond market.

---

[11] ADB's investment in AC Energy was $20 million, approved and signed in January 2019; and $98 million (3 billion Thai baht) in Energy Absolute, approved and signed in September 2019.

▲ **A communications student in the Philippines.** ADB's equity investments help improve the access, quality, and affordability of education (photo by Al Benavente for ADB).

POST-COMPLETION EVALUATION OF TRANSACTIONS

At the time of project completion, PSOD prepares extended annual review reports (XARRs) for transactions. These XARRs evaluate the success of transactions based on the development results achieved, investment profitability, work quality, and additionality. These findings are validated by ADB's Independent Evaluation Department (IED).

The XARRs prepared in 2019 cover 23 completed transactions approved between 2005 to 2015. Seventeen of these were rated *successful* (Figure 18).

Of the six projects that were rated *less than successful* or *unsuccessful,* four were private equity funds approved between 2005 and 2008. These funds were affected by a set of external factors, including the adverse timing of some of the funds' launch and fundraising, which coincided with the global financial crisis of 2008, stock market volatility, and currency devaluation.

Figure 18: Ratings for Completed Transactions, 2019

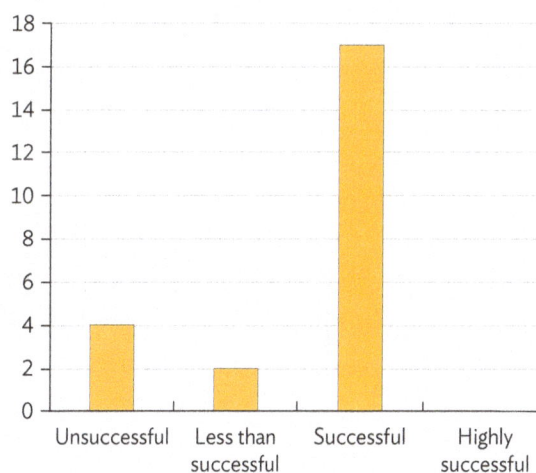

Source: Asian Development Bank (Private Sector Operations Department).

Some internal factors such as team composition, limited fund management experience, changes in investment strategy, and legal and regulatory matters also contributed to low performance of these funds.

Awards Received by ADB, Its Investees, and Transactions

ADB	Asian Development Bank	IJGlobal Awards 2019	**Asia Pacific Development Finance Institution of the Year**
	Asia-Pacific Remote Broadband Internet Satellite Project (Regional)	IJGlobal Awards 2019	**Asia Pacific Telecoms Deal of the Year**
	Floating Solar Energy Project (Viet Nam)	IJGlobal Awards 2019	**Asia Pacific Innovation Deal of the Year**
	Eastern Economic Corridor Independent Power Project (Thailand)	IJGlobal Awards 2019	**Asia Pacific Power Deal of the Year**
	Jawa-1 Liquefied Natural Gas-to-Power Project (Indonesia)	ASIAN POWER AWARDS 2019	**Natural Gas-Fired Power Project of the Year (Gold)**
	Rantau Dedap Geothermal Power Project (Indonesia)	ASIAN POWER AWARDS 2019	**Geothermal Power Project of the Year (Gold)**
	Southern Thailand Waste-to-Energy Project (Thailand)	ASIAN POWER AWARDS 2019	**Biomass Power Project of the Year (Gold)**
	Thailand Green Bond Project (Thailand)	ASIAN POWER AWARDS 2019	**Solar Power Project of the Year**

Awards Received by ADB, Its Investees, and Transactions

	Project	Award Body	Award
	Energy Absolute Green Bond for Wind Power Project (Thailand)	**PFI AWARDS 2019** Project Finance International (PFI Awards 2019)	**Local Currency Deal of the Year**
	Upper Trishuli-1 Hydropower Project (Nepal)	**PFI AWARDS 2019** Project Finance International (PFI Awards 2019)	**DFI Deal of the Year**
	Eastern Economic Corridor Independent Power Project (Thailand)	**PFI AWARDS 2019** Project Finance International (PFI Awards 2019)	**Asia Pacific Power Deal of the Year**
	Jawa-1 Liquefied Natural Gas-to-Power Project (Indonesia)	ASSET ASIAN AWARDS 2019 THE Asset TRIPLE A — Infrastructure Awards 2019	**Power Deal of the Year/ PPP Project of the Year**
	Eastern Indonesia Renewable Energy Project (Indonesia)	ASSET ASIAN AWARDS 2019 THE Asset TRIPLE A — Infrastructure Awards 2019	**Renewable Energy Deal of the Year – Solar and Wind**
	Rantua Dedap Geothermal Power Project (Indonesia)	ASSET ASIAN AWARDS 2019 THE Asset TRIPLE A — Infrastructure Awards 2019	**Renewable Energy Deal of the Year – Geothermal**
	Thailand Green Bond Project (Thailand)	ASSET ASIAN AWARDS 2019 THE Asset TRIPLE A — Infrastructure Awards 2019	**Green Financing of the Year**

Measuring ADB's Private Sector Operations Contributions to the Sustainable Development Goals

SDGs	Indicators	ADB Results as of 2019
1 NO POVERTY	Number of people employed	319,743
	MSME beneficiaries	33.2 million
	SME beneficiaries	826,591
2 ZERO HUNGER	Number of farmers reached	1.5 million
	Agricultural production (tons)	1.4 million
3 GOOD HEALTH AND WELL-BEING	Number of hospitals constructed and/or expanded	12
	Number of hospital beds purchased	1,818
	Number of patients served	8.8 million
4 QUALITY EDUCATION	Number of students reached	35,568
5 GENDER EQUALITY	Women-owned MSME beneficiaries	24.6 million
	Women-owned SME beneficiaries	752,620
	Number of women employed	84,407
	Number of female farmers reached	5,240
6 CLEAN WATER AND SANITATION	Households with access to energy	37,875
	Households with access to water	769,166
	Potable water produced (m^3)	874.8 million
	Wastewater treated (m^3)	1.1 billion
7 AFFORDABLE AND CLEAN ENERGY	Power delivered (GWh)	36,358
8 DECENT WORK AND ECONOMIC GROWTH	Number of people trained	422,830
	Number of people employed	319,743
9 INDUSTRY, INNOVATION, AND INFRASTRUCTURE	Volume of cargo processed and/or transported (tons)	216 million
	Number of passengers reached	50 million
	Number of telecom towers built	8,019
	Number of power transmission towers built	1,714
10 REDUCED INEQUALITIES	Number of indigenous people employed	2,926
11 SUSTAINABLE CITIES AND COMMUNITIES	Households with access to energy	37,875
	Households with access to water	769,166
	Potable water produced (m^3)	874.8 million
	Wastewater treated (m^3)	1.1 billion
	Number of passengers reached	50 million
13 CLIMATE ACTION	Greenhouse gas emissions reduced (tCO_2e)	30.7 million
17 PARTNERSHIPS FOR THE GOALS	Government revenues ($)	9.5 billion
	Domestic purchases ($)	13.8 billion

ADB = Asian Development Bank; GWh = gigawatt-hour; m^3 = cubic meter; MSMEs = micro, small, and medium-sized enterprises; SMEs = small and medium-sized enterprises; tCO_2e = tons of carbon dioxide equivalent.

Source: Asian Development Bank (Private Sector Operations Department).

www.ingramcontent.com/pod-product-compliance
Lightning Source LLC
Chambersburg PA
CBHW040146200326

41519CB00035B/7616